FORCEPS DELIVERIES

Obstetrics and Gynecology Series
Edited by Claude E. Heaton, M.D.

CONSULTING OBSTETRICIAN AND GYNECOLOGIST: Muhlenberg Hospital, Plainfield, N. J.; Greenwich Hospital, Greenwich, Conn.; St. Josephs Hospital, Stamford, Conn.; Mt. Vernon Hospital, Mt. Vernon, N. Y.; Perth Amboy General Hospital, Perth Amboy, N. J.; Surgeon General, U. S. Army; Polyclinic Hospital, New York, N. Y.; New York Hospital, New York, N. Y.; Norwalk Hospital, Norwalk, Conn.

CONSULTING OBSTETRICIAN: Englewood Hospital, Englewood, N. J.; United Hospital, Port Chester, N. Y.; Harlem Hospital, New York, N. Y.

DIPLOMATE AMERICAN BOARD OF OBSTETRICS AND GYNECOLOGY

FELLOW AMERICAN ASSOCIATION OF OBSTETRICIANS AND GYNECOLOGISTS

FELLOW AMERICAN COLLEGE OF OBSTETRICIANS AND GYNECOLOGISTS

FELLOW AMERICAN COLLEGE OF SURGEONS

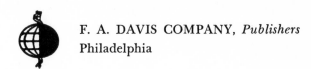

F. A. DAVIS COMPANY, *Publishers*
Philadelphia

FORCEPS DELIVERIES

Edition 2

EDWARD H. DENNEN, M.D.

97
ILLUSTRATIONS

The drawings were done by Mr. Alfred Fineberg, Medical Artist, Columbia University, New York

Professor Emeritus, Obstetrics and Gynecology, New York Polyclinic Medical School and Hospital. ☐ Professor of Clinical Obstetrics and Gynecology, Cornell Medical College.

To My Wife

LEILA HEDGES DENNEN

Foreword

In obstetrical textbooks and in most delivery rooms, explicit instruction in the use of forceps is meager. The beginner, generally under scant supervision, must learn from experience.

Safety requires that one have a thorough understanding of forceps and a rationale in their use. Experience then will be more valuable and skill more quickly acquired.

The author has described the various forceps, given their indications and has told and shown how to use them. His effort is based on a large experience, not only in operative work, but also in teaching at the delivery table and on the manikin.

The student of obstetrical surgery should find much help in this practical book.

Everett M. Hawks, M.D.

Preface

The continued interest in the book and the passage of time are responsible for this second edition of "Forceps Deliveries."

A number of additions and alterations have been made in the text of the second edition, for clarification and completeness. The more lengthy additions deal with pertinent subjects not included originally or developed recently.

In the second edition, as in the first, allied subjects have not been included in order to preserve the original intent of limiting the discussions, as far as possible, to forceps deliveries.

New illustrations have been included in two of the chapters.

Some of the new instruments are discussed from the viewpoint of their advantages and disadvantages in the selection of a forceps for the individual delivery.

Of special importance is the detailed consideration of the different methods of application of the Kielland forceps. Although the inversion method is the standard one for most deliveries with the Kielland forceps, in certain conditions this method is contraindicated, if not impossible. In some of these situations, either the wandering or the direct method is indicated.

In the chapter on the choice of instruments the results in a sizable series (10,405) of consecutive forceps deliveries have been added. Mortality figures are given in correlation with the high, mid, low mid and low application of forceps.

Finally, the list of references has been reviewed and pertinent additions made.

Edward H. Dennen

Table of Contents

Introduction

DETAILED INSTRUCTION in the use of the various types of obstetrical forceps is difficult to obtain. The old adage, taught for years, "Learn how to use one type of forceps and use it well," has done much to retard the interest in other types despite their admitted advantages under certain conditions.

Designers of forceps and their satellites and students, who became teachers, taught only the use of their favorite type. Other types were ignored except to emphasize their disadvantages. The numerous types in general use show that there is no universal forceps. Many an operator has experienced the sense of relief and the thrill of success following the use of one type of forceps after failure with another type on the same case. There were reasons present why one pair of forceps succeeded after another had failed. These reasons represented the advantages of the former and the disadvantages of the latter.

With the advent of special types of forceps, more advantages appeared as well as more disadvantages. Also, different technics of application and traction were required. A thorough knowledge of the advantages and disadvantages of the various types of forceps, and the technics of their use

1

will eliminate many of the bad results following blind faith in one type, or the "trial and error" method.

The ultimate object of this book is to show that there is a choice of instrument in delivery with forceps, depending upon the existing conditions; that one should choose the type of forceps that suits the case rather than try to make all cases fit one type of forceps. To help in accomplishing this object, the various types of forceps are classified. Their style of construction is stated. The advantages and disadvantages of each are emphasized. A detailed description of the technic of the application and traction for each type is given, with reasons for success or failure and pitfalls to be avoided.

A classification of forceps operations according to the station of the head in the pelvis is stated. This is based on the four major planes of the pelvis, each of which serves as a label for the forceps operation done at the corresponding level in the pelvis. The term "low-mid forceps" is introduced for operations done on a head arrested at the plane of least pelvic dimensions. This divides the long distance between high and low into mid and low-mid, and the advantages and the exceptions are given.

The eight positions in which the fetal occiput may lie at the time of operation are taken up in order. The different operations and maneuvers and choice of instrument for each position are described. For example: An R. O. P. may be handled by manual rotation to anterior, followed by application of the forceps; by instrumental rotation, or by a combination of manual and instrumental rotation. Manual rotation includes a description of the Pomeroy maneuver.

Instrumental rotation describes the modified Scanzoni maneuver with the double application of the Elliot type of forceps; the "key in lock" maneuver with multiple applications of the DeLee-Simpson forceps; and the single application of the special type of forceps, the Kielland and the Barton, with mention of modifications of the classical type such as the Mann, the Miseo, the Jacobs, and the La Breck, and of the special type, the Laufe.

The combined manual and instrumental rotation describes the wandering maneuver for application of the anterior blade of the classical instrument.

In certain types of pelves, anterior rotation is contraindicated. Then the head is delivered as an occiput posterior with a Simpson type of forceps having a good pelvic curve and good axis traction.

Face presentation in its various positions is covered with the use of the Kielland forceps. This includes the special technic of the "upside down" direct application for a posterior chin. Also, the aftercoming head of a breech delivery is handled with the Piper forceps, specially designed for this purpose.

Although the object of this book is to show there is a choice of instrument in delivery with forceps, the subject matter deals with a detailed discussion of how to use forceps— *all forceps in general use.* The choice takes into consideration the advantages of one type over another under existing conditions. The more complicated the case, the more factors are present to influence the choice.

In the text it is shown that in one not uncommon situa-

tion, namely, a flat pelvis with a transverse arrest of the head
(especially one with a straight sacrum), only one type of
forceps can be used with any degree of safety, the Barton.
(An exception may be the Miseo forceps which is not in general use.) In fact, the classical instruments often cannot even
be applied, or if applied, the result is usually extreme trauma
or failure. Many of the bad results blamed on the Kielland
forceps occurred in such cases. This caused discredit and
prejudice to be cast upon one of the most valuable obstetrical
instruments for posterior positions, deep transverse arrests,
and face presentations. Yet in many localities the use of the
Barton forceps is not taught, although they have been available since 1925.

The public eye is directed toward obstetrics in regard to
the improving of results and to an increasing demand for
relief of pain in labor. Both of these call for knowledge and
skill on the part of the physician. More analgesia increases
the number of operative deliveries. A good result depends
largely upon the ability of the operator. A properly chosen
and well executed forceps delivery does not increase the risk
of a bad result. Nor does the operator, in the average case,
have to be one of exceptional skill provided he has had
detailed training in the use of forceps, follows the rules, and
knows his limitations.

During the thirteen years from 1941 through 1953 on the
service at the N. Y. Polyclinic Hospital, there was a total of
9237 forceps operations performed. This included all types.
The gross infant mortality (fetal and neonatal) was ninety-
four or 1.01 per cent. The corrected mortality was fifty-six

or 0.60 per cent (thirty-eight were monsters or macerated babies). The morbidity was seventy-nine or 0.85 per cent. During the same period, there were 4583 spontaneous births with an infant mortality of 135 or 2.9 per cent. This was corrected to fifty-three or 1.15 per cent by removing eighty-two monsters and macerated babies. The morbidity was forty-eight or 1.04 per cent. Despite the fact that most of the difficult cases were in the operative group, the infant mortality and the morbidity in this group were considerably less than in the spontaneous group. There were more than 100 different operators, varying in experience, from the obstetrical surgeon to the junior intern.

To get the best results in a forceps operation, there are certain fundamental rules which must be strictly followed. First, it must be considered as a surgical procedure and, as such, it should be given the thought, attention, dignity, and respect accorded to any other branch of surgery. It should be done by a trained, coordinated operating team consisting of, in addition to the operator, an assistant—the resident or intern (two, if retraction is necessary and the baby needs special attention)—a trained anesthetist, a scrub nurse, and a circulating nurse. To be short of help in an emergency—and one might develop at any time—is a dangerous and harrowing experience. A forceps delivery certainly deserves as much trained attention as is given the average vaginal plastic operation, or even that given to a diagnostic curettage. Any operator does a better job, with less risk and less effort, if he has good assistance.

The delivery room should be fully equipped and set up,

at all times, ready for immediate use. The instrument table should have on it a sufficient number and variety of instruments to handle almost any complication ordinarily dealt with in the delivery room. This eliminates needless waste of precious time, sending elsewhere for something in an emergency. A delivery table which permits lowering of the legs during delivery of the baby's head over the perineum minimizes the risk of a third degree laceration, especially in the presence of a median episiotomy.

Equipment for hypodermic, intramuscular, and intravenous therapy and the usual medications, should always be in the room. Glucose and saline solutions should always be handy to the delivery room, and a laboratory available for blood transfusion on short notice. In this respect a preliminary blood typing and Rh factor determination, done on the patient at an earlier date, are definitely advantageous.

The anesthesia equipment, including that for suction and resuscitation of both mother and baby, should be complete and serviceable. This requires constant inspection, as it is most distressing to find, when about to use it, that the airway is missing, or the oxygen tank is empty, or the laryngoscope gives no light.

The intern, before being allowed to perform a forceps operation, should be given a series of painstaking lectures on the subject. He should be drilled in detail, repeatedly, on the manikin and he should assist at numerous operations which, in turn, should be reviewed on the manikin. Then when his instructor is satisfied that he is properly prepared, the intern is allowed to do an easy case under direct supervision. The amount and type of work that he does should then increase rapidly in proportion to his ability to handle it.

Finally, the operator should be familiar with the advantages and disadvantages of the different types of forceps and the technic of their use. This permits him to choose the type which is best suited for the individual case.

E. H. D.

OBSTETRICS & GYNECOLOGY

FORCEPS DELIVERIES

CHAPTER 1

Prerequisites for Forceps Deliveries

INDICATIONS for forceps deliveries vary from extreme danger signals in the mother or child to a prophylactic procedure.

The major prerequisites of a forceps delivery are of vital importance and should be emphasized. These are: the head should be engaged; the cervix should be fully dilated; the exact position of the head should be determined; the type of pelvis should be known; the operator should be familiar with the advantages and disadvantages of the different types of instruments and the technic of their use. Exceptions to these requirements exist, but they are rare and such circumstances which will warrant the ignoring of these rules will not be encountered frequently. When present, they require expert attention.

An unengaged head in almost all instances is considered to be a contraindication for a forceps delivery. The risk to both mother and baby makes it unwarranted to attempt such

11

a procedure. The lower the head is in the pelvis, the easier and safer will be the operation.

Full dilation of the cervix in most cases is essential to success in a forceps delivery. In complicated cases, in which forceps delivery is indicated, an effaced, flaccid, nonresistant, negotiable rim of a cervix may be brought to full dilation digitally, or if resistant and non-negotiable, by judicious use of cervical incisions. However, these procedures are distinctly contraindicated if the head is not well down in the pelvis and if the cervix is not completely effaced.

A correct diagnosis of the position of the head is necessary in order to get a correct application and proper traction with the forceps. Most heads should be delivered in the anterior, O.A. position with a correct application of the forceps. This reduces the effort necessary for delivery and minimizes the injuries which may accompany it. Heads not in the O.A. position are rotated to it, either manually or instrumentally. Therefore, an error in diagnosis of position is followed by an incorrect application of the forceps and improper traction, and the accompanying risk of serious injuries. Not infrequently the diagnosis of position is difficult to make. Continued practice and constant alertness are important factors in maintaining a high percentage of correct diagnosis. This problem may be simplified if attention is concentrated on the sutures rather than the size and shape of a fontanelle, which may be distorted or obscured by molding or edema. Three sutures, the two halves of the lamboidal joined by the sagittal, forming a letter Y, indicate the posterior fontanelle, hence, an inverted Y to the left is an L.O.P., an upright Y to the right is an R.O.A. and a horizontal Y to the left is an L.O.T. (Fig. 1). In case of doubt the sagittal suture should be traced to its opposite end. Identification of the anterior fontanelle is more readily made, since it is the junction of four lines meeting in the form of a cross. These lines are the two halves of the coronal suture, the sagittal and the frontal.

Occasionally, on tracing the sagittal suture throughout its length, it will be found to be curved like the letter U with its most dependent portion closer to the sacrum than the symphysis. Also, each fontanelle is in an anterior quadrant of the pelvis. This should be recognized as an anterior parietal presentation caused by anterior asynclitism (Fig. 2). Thus, what was originally thought to be an anterior position of the head because the posterior fontanelle was found in an anterior quadrant, now will be diagnosed as a transverse position. Less frequently, the opposite situation will be found. In posterior asynclitism (Fig. 3) the posterior parietal bone presents with the inverted U of the sagittal suture closer to the symphysis than the sacrum and its extremities dipping into the posterior quadrants. This is likewise a transverse position and is found usually in a flat pelvis with an unengaged head.

If only one end of the sagittal suture can be felt and it is thought to terminate in the posterior fontanelle, a check may be made. By sweeping the examining fingers over the supposed occipital bone from one side of the Y to the other (the two halves of the lamboidal suture) another suture line, a continuation of the sagittal suture, may be felt dividing the intervening space. If so, it makes a fourth line leading to the same fontanelle and is, therefore, the frontal suture leading

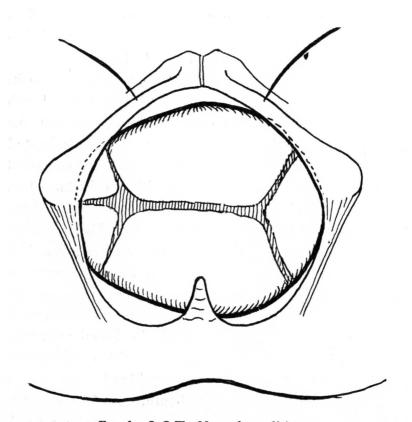

FIG. 1. L.O.T. Normal synclitism.

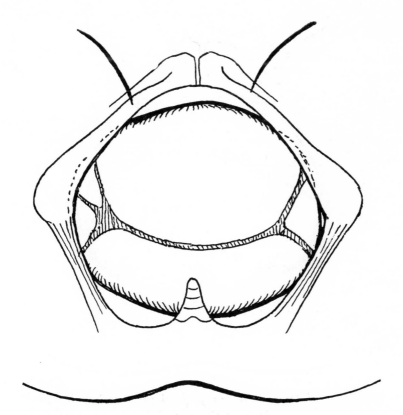

FIG. 2. L.O.T. Anterior parietal presentation due to anterior asynclitism.

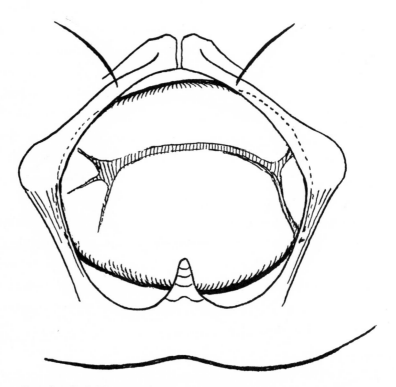

FIG. 3. L.O.T. Posterior parietal presentation due to the posterior asynclitism.

into the anterior fontanelle. If doubt still persists, the posterior ear may be felt for, to establish the exact position of the occiput. However, this procedure is reserved as a last resort because of the risk of displacement and backward rotation of the head. It has been said that a displaced head will come down again. Unfortunately, this does not always occur, at least, not in as favorable a position. Thus, the accomplishment of hours of labor may be lost. Many of the technical difficulties of a forceps delivery may be avoided by not displacing the head. Occasionally, these difficulties are so great as to force the operator to abandon further attempts at delivery with forceps in favor of some other procedure, originally considered unindicated or more hazardous.

A knowledge of the type and size of the pelvis is important because it helps the operator rule out cephalopelvic disproportion, which is a contraindication to a forceps delivery. Also it enables him to utilize the best available diameters for traction. X-ray pelvimetry is an invaluable aid in diagnosis, but to it must be added clinical experience, especially when dealing with deformities of the lower half of the pelvis. In some cases of flat pelvis the type of asynclitism must be recognized and corrected. In pelves with a narrow transverse diameter throughout (anthropoid), also those with a male outlet (android), it must be decided whether or not to rotate an occiput posterior position to anterior before extraction. In some cases, with prominent ischial spines or a prominent coccyx, it is necessary to rotate a head which is in the direct occiput anterior position, back to the anterior oblique. Traction is then applied in this diameter of the pelvis until the head has passed the point of obstruction.

Obstetrical forceps in a general way may be divided into two types, classical and special. The classical type is composed of instruments which follow a style of construction and usage accepted as standard for years. The special type comprises more recently developed instruments which differ markedly from the standard in principles of construction and technic of use. Some instruments have special advantages under certain conditions, others are definitely contraindicated. Some fit the shape of molded heads, others round heads. With some, a more accurate application can be obtained with less manipulation. Others give a better line of traction. A knowledge of the advantages, disadvantages, and technic of the use of the various types of forceps permits the operator to choose the type best suited for the case.

CHAPTER 2

A Classification of Forceps Operations According to Station of Head in Pelvis

THE SYSTEM of classification now in use describing the station of the head in the pelvis when forceps are applied is far from satisfactory.

The long distance from low to mid pelvis and the short distance from mid to high pelvis have led to numerous errors in classification. The logical approach to the problem is to relate the station of the head (the biparietal diameter) to the four major planes of the pelvis (Fig. 4). They are: the plane of the inlet (superior strait) which is bounded by the promontory of the sacrum and the upper, inner border of the symphysis; the plane of greatest pelvic dimensions (midplane) which extends between the middle of the inner border of the symphysis and the junction of the second and third sacral vertebrae; the plane of least pelvic dimensions (plane of ischial spines), which is bounded anteroposteriorly by the lower, inner border of the symphysis and the sacrococcygeal joint and laterally by the ischial spines; the plane of the outlet, quadrilateral in shape, which is bounded by the sacrococcygeal joint, the ischial tuberosities and the inferior border of the symphysis. The corresponding operative deliveries should be entitled high, mid, low-mid, and low forceps.

A *high* forceps delivery (Fig. 5) is one in which the biparietal diameter is in the inlet or superior strait of the pelvis and the leading bony point of the head is just above the plane of the ischial spines. Anything higher should be labeled a forceps to an unengaged head.

A *mid* forceps delivery is one done on a head, the leading bony part of which is at or just below the plane of the ischial spines with the biparietal diameter below the superior strait. The head nearly fills the hollow of the sacrum.

A *low-mid* forceps delivery is one in which the biparietal diameter is at or below the plane of the ischial spines with the leading bony point within a finger's breadth of the perineum between contractions. The head completely fills the hollow of the sacrum.

A *low* forceps delivery is one in which the bony head is on the perineum and its leading point is visible between contractions. The biparietal diameter is judged to be in the plane of the outlet, with the sagittal suture in or nearly coinciding with the anteroposterior diameter of the outlet.

The average case fits into one of these categories. However, exceptions must be made for extreme molding, extension, and asynclitism and for deformities of the pelvis which

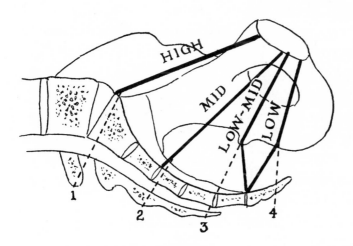

1. Plane of Inlet
2. Plane of greatest pelvic dimensions
3. Plane of least pelvic dimensions
4. Plane of Outlet

FIG. 4.   Four major planes of the pelvis.

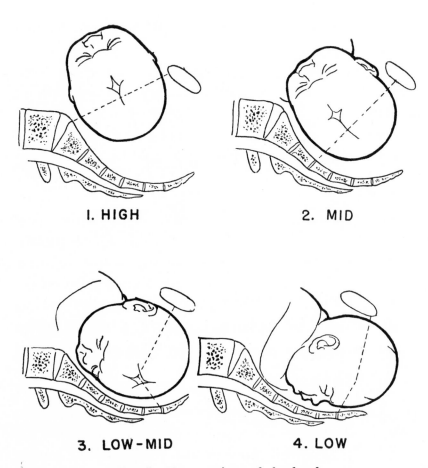

1. HIGH 2. MID

3. LOW-MID 4. LOW

Fig. 5. Four stations of the head.

predispose to these conditions. In such instances the biparietal diameter usually is at a higher level in its relationship
to the leading point of the head than in the average case.
Unless these variable factors are taken into consideration
errors in diagnosis of the exact station are frequent.

Extreme molding lengthens the long axis of the head.
Hence the biparietal diameter is at a correspondingly greater
distance from the leading point (Fig. 6). The estimation of
this distance is of the greatest importance, since the biparietal
diameter is the widest diameter of the fetal head which must
pass through the maternal pelvis and its level designates the
true station of the head.

With the leading point at the plane of the ischial spines
the biparietal diameter may be at the inlet. Consequently,
what is thought to be the head in mid station is in reality at
a high station. Also, in cases with the leading point on the
perineum, the biparietal diameter may be at or above the
ischial spines. What is often thought to be an easy low forceps
delivery is later proved to be a difficult delivery of a head at
or above the low-mid station.

Faulty attitudes such as varying degrees of extension of
the head, including the extremes of brow and face presentations, and the abnormal attitude of asynclitism, influence the
level of the biparietal diameter with relation to the leading
point.

In extensions of the head, the biparietal diameter is
farther from the leading point than in normal occipital presentations (Fig. 7). Hence, the station of the biparietal diameter is higher than would be expected in an occiput presenta-

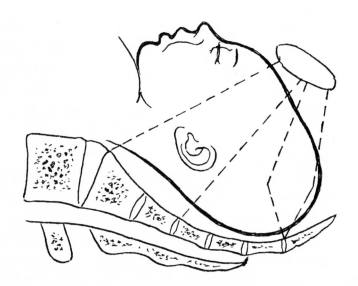

EXTREME MOLDING
MID O.P.

Fig. 6.

tion with the leading point at the same level. The greater the extension, the more the variation. In asynclitism, either the anterior or the posterior parietal bone is presenting (Fig. 8). Therefore, one extremity of the biparietal is considerably lower than the other. The actual station of the head depends upon the level of the "pivot point" which is the midpoint of the biparietal diameter. The location of this point must be judged by the degree of asynclitism and the level of the leading point. The more asynclitic the head, the greater the chances of error in diagnosis of station. One is apt to consider the head at a lower level than is the case.

Clinically, this is more frequent in asynclitism with the anterior parietal bone well under the symphysis, and the hollow of the sacrum empty. When the posterior parietal bone presents, the anterior pelvis is usually empty, since the anterior parietal bone overrides the symphysis and can be palpated above it.

The degree of asynclitism can best be determined by the shape and the location of the sagittal suture. The greater the degree of asynclitism, the more the shape of the sagittal suture changes from a straight line to the shape of the letter "U". With the anterior parietal bone presenting, the "U" is upright and the most dependent portion of the "U" becomes closer to the sacrum and farther away from the symphysis as the asynclitism increases. In a posterior parietal bone presentation, the "U" is inverted and the superior point of its base is closer to the symphysis than to the sacrum.

Deformities of the pelvis may predispose to and accentuate molding, extensions, and asynclitism. These deformities may

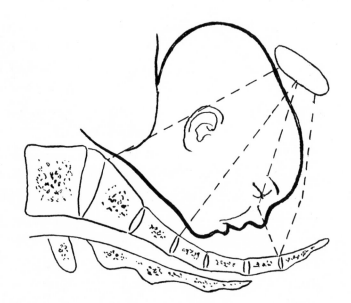

HIGH POST. CHIN

Fig. 7.

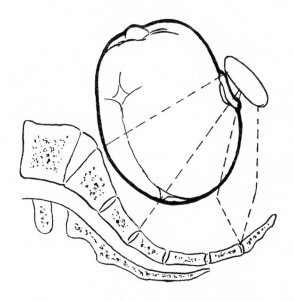

ANT. PARIETAL PRESENTATION
HIGH L.O.T.

Fig. 8

involve any of the major planes of the pelvis and, consequently, affect the accuracy of the diagnosis of station.

At the inlet or high-plane, molding is common in small
gynecoid and android pelves, especially with posterior positions. Asynclitism and extensions, even to the degree of face
presentation, are frequently found in platypelloid pelves.
With the head arrested at this level, the common mistake is
to consider the head engaged when in reality the biparietal is
above the inlet.

Deformities of the plane of greatest pelvic dimensions or
mid-plane, carry with them similar factors as those of the
inlet, and affect molding, extensions, and asynclitism. A transverse contraction in the anthropoid and android types frequently leads to a posterior position with more than average
molding. A contracted anteroposterior diameter, due to a
straight sacrum or a forward jutting sacral vertebra, leads to
a transverse position with extension and asynclitism. Hence,
most of these cases should be classed as high instead of mid,
as the biparietal diameter is usually at the inlet. This knowledge should influence the operator to avoid the dangerous
high forceps operation.

In the plane of least pelvic dimensions, the plane of the
ischial spines, or low-mid-plane, the greatest percentage of
dystocias is encountered. The type of pelvis that carries with
it the most difficulty at this level is the android. Here the
molding is accentuated. It may be so extreme as to have the
leading point touching the perineum when the biparietal
diameter is still above the ischial spines. The common error
in diagnosis in such cases is to label the operation low forceps

instead of mid. In this extreme situation, with the biparietal above the spines, the operation cannot be classed even as low-mid.

The deformities of the low-plane or outlet, particularly those with a funnel outlet, predispose to posterior positions and excessive molding. Here again, if the diagnosis of station were made on the leading point alone, the delivery would be classed as a low forceps. When correctly made on the biparietal diameter it is a low-mid forceps.

Determination of the exact level of the biparietal diameter may be difficult to make, except on certain unengaged heads. In all complicated cases a vaginal examination is essential in determining the true picture. It is important that the phrase "at the spines" is correctly understood. When a leading point is at the spines, it has reached a plane that includes the ischial spines laterally and the sacrococcygeal junction posteriorly. In such a situation the hollow of the sacrum is nearly filled by the head. The common error is to feel the fetal head in the anterior part of the pelvis, and to consider the vertex at the spines without investigating further to see whether the hollow of the sacrum is empty. The difference may be between a head that is in mid pelvis and one that is high or unengaged. X-ray study in labor is a valuable aid especially in complicated cases. A sideview gives the exact level of the biparietal diameter. Also, it may show a previously unrecognized deformity of the sacrum to be the cause of dystocia. In the average case it can be assumed that the biparietal diameter is located at a certain level, depending on the level of the leading point, as has been indicated. But in cases with extreme molding, abnormal attitudes, and in deformed pelves predisposing to these conditions, it automatically should be placed at least at the next higher plane.

The advantages of this method are many. It is a definite means of classification and is self explanatory, in that the stations of the head correspond with the four major planes of the pelvis and the operative deliveries from these stations are similarly named. Honest and human errors in diagnosis of station are reduced to a minimum.

Attempts at a forceps delivery on the unengaged head and on all but the extremely rare high head can be avoided. At the same time, it is realized that visual evidence of the fetal scalp at the perineum does not necessarily mean an easy "low" forceps delivery. Without a systematized classification, there is a great void between the low forceps, in which the head is visible, and the "mid" forceps, which may be anything from an easy low-mid forceps to a complicated delivery of a head at the inlet. This is one reason why the valuable true mid forceps operation has fallen into discredit.

CHAPTER 3

Classical Instruments

Construction

THE CLASSICAL instrument consists of two blades each connected to a handle by a shank. The blade may be fenestrated or solid and is connected to the shank at an angle anteriorly, which corresponds to the curve of the pelvis. Beside the pelvic curve, the blade has a lateral curve corresponding to that of the side of the child's head, known as the cephalic curve. The tip of the blade is the toe, and the portion of the blade attached to the shank at the posterior lip of the fenestration is the heel. At or near the junction of the handle and the shank is the lock. Originally, forceps had no lock but as the modern instrument passed through its various stages of development, there appeared fixed locks, semifixed locks, set screw locks, and cross bar locks. The pendulum is swinging away from the fixed lock and at the present time the sliding lock is in vogue. If the proper type of forceps is selected and correctly applied, there rarely will be necessity for a fixed lock to keep the blades from slipping.

31

Types of Classical Forceps

The type of classical instrument is determined mainly by its shank. In order to select the proper forceps it must be known that there are two types of the classical instrument.

Elliot Type

The Elliot type of instrument has *overlapping* shanks which impart a short *round* cephalic curve to the blades. Due to the overlapping of the shanks, the blades must curve widely in order to attain a distance between them which is necessary for the accommodation of a child's head that has a biparietal diameter of about 9.5 cm. This bulging at the heels resulting in a round cephalic curve, makes the Elliot type of forceps the instrument of choice for application to round unmolded heads. The Elliot, the Tucker-McLane, and the Bailey-Williamson forceps are examples of the Elliot type (Fig. 9).

Simpson Type

The Simpson type of forceps has parallel *separated* shanks which result in a *long, tapering* cephalic curve. This type of cephalic curve makes the blade fit better on the long molded head. The Simpson, DeLee, DeWees, Good, Tarnier, Irving, Haig-Ferguson, and Hawks-Dennen forceps are examples of the Simpson type (Fig. 9).

Application

All applications must be cephalic. There is no longer any place for the so-called pelvic application and this term should be discarded.

In the application of forceps, the place of application

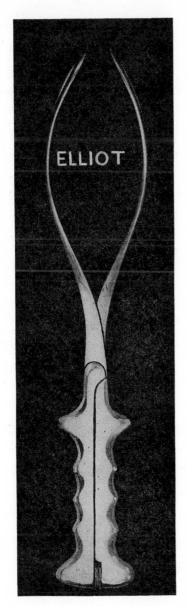 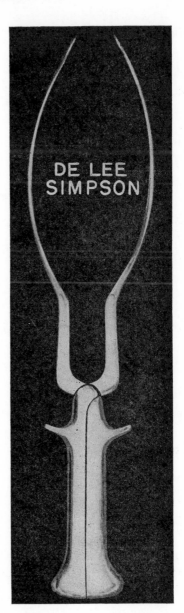

Fig. 9.

of the blade and the shape of the head must be considered
In a true cephalic application, the blades should fit the head
as accurately as possible. They should lie evenly against
the sides of the head, reaching from the parietal bosses to
and beyond the malar eminences covering symmetrically the
spaces between the orbits and the ears (Fig. 10). There
should be no extra pressure at any one point. A correct
application is essential. It prevents injury to the head because the blades fit the head accurately and pressure is evenly
distributed; the pressure is on the least vulnerable areas;
the increased diameter of the head, due to the thickness of
the blades, is at the narrowest place, thereby minimizing the
force necessary for delivery. It lessens injury to the mother
because the head advances in the proper attitude of flexion.
It is vital to the technic of delivery because it enables the
operator to know the exact position of the head, thereby
permitting him to use the most favorable diameters. These
conditions are not fulfilled by the undesirable brow-mastoid
application.

On molded heads, the best application is obtained with
blades which have a long, tapering cephalic curve as in the
Simpson type. Those with a short, full curve of the Elliot
type do not fit evenly, causing pressure points and often are
not anchored below the malar eminences with consequent
cutting or slipping.

Diagnosis of Proper Application

There are three landmarks to be considered in checking
the diagnosis of a proper application. They are the posterior
fontanelle, the sagittal suture, and the fenestration.

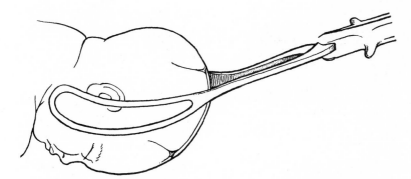

FIG. 10. True cephalic (biparietal, bimalar) application.

The *posterior fontanelle* in anterior positions of the head should be one finger's breadth anterior to the plane of the shanks. The fontanelle is also equidistant from the sides of the blades. If the posterior fontanelle is more than one finger's breadth anterior to the plane of the shanks, the blades are too far back on the face. The head usually is not well flexed and traction will cause it to extend further. If the posterior fontanelle is less than one finger's breadth anterior to the plane of the shanks, traction will cause the head to flex. With the posterior fontanelle not in the proper relation to the plane of the shanks, the pivot point of the head will not be in the center of the blades.

The pivot point or the midpoint of the biparietal diameter of the head should lie in the midpoint of a line connecting the widest diameter of the cephalic curve of the blades. If the forceps are applied so that the pivot point of the head is not in the center of the blades, traction causes the head to become either overextended or overflexed, usually the former, depending upon whether the posterior fontanelle is more or less than one finger's breadth anterior to the plane of the shanks. The pivot point cannot be checked, but it may be assumed to be in the center of the blades if the posterior fontanelle is one finger's breadth anterior to the plane of the shanks and equidistant from the sides of the blades.

The sagittal suture throughout its entire length is perpendicular to the middle of the plane of the shanks. If the sagittal suture curves to one side it suggests a brow-mastoid application. If it is parallel to, but does not coincide with, the mid-perpendicular of the plane of the shanks, the appli-

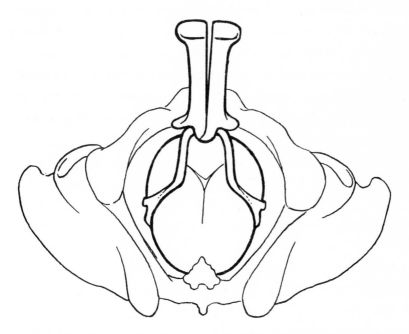

FIG. 11. Correct application — according to the three checks.

cation is asynclitic. This situation cannot be corrected when due to the flattening of one side of the head as in a flat pelvis.

After the blades are applied, the *fenestration* can barely be felt, if at all. Not more than the tip of one finger can be inserted into the fenestration in advance of the head. If too much of the fenestration can be palpated, the blade has not been inserted far enough to be well anchored below the malar eminence, or the head is very small (Fig. 11).

It is difficult to tell whether the forceps fit the head evenly without causing unequal pressure. However, it can be assumed that they do if a Simpson type is used on a molded head and an Elliot type on a round head.

CHAPTER 4

Technic of Application

THE PATIENT, in the lithotomy position under obstetrical anesthesia is prepared, draped, and catheterized in the usual manner. Skilled administration of an anesthetic by a trained person is essential. The most skilfully performed forceps delivery may be ruined by a laryngospasm or a respiratory paralysis. Except for cesarean operations, the choice of anesthesia induction, on a service with a well organized anesthesia department, is by general inhalation.

Spinal, perineal, pudendal block, and intravenous anesthesia are reserved for selected cases or when good general anesthesia is unavailable. The perineum, when resistant, is ironed out with a lubricant, sufficiently to permit introduction of the blades. While ironing out the perineum, fundal pressure is exerted so as not to displace the head. Maintenance of station cannot be overemphasized because the higher the head, the more complicated is the operation. If intact, the membranes are ruptured in order to facilitate the diagnosis of position and avoid the possibility of premature separation of the placenta during traction. A vaginal examination is then

39

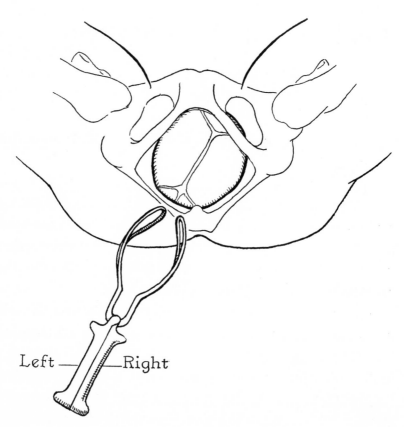

FIG. 12. Orientation for L.O.A.

made to check the exact position of the head. Then the blades are identified by holding them locked with the pelvic curve up, directed toward the patient in the position in which they will be when applied to the sides of the head (Fig. 12). The left hand of the operator automatically grasps the handle of the left blade and the right hand grasps the handle of the right blade.

There are four cardinal points to remember when the occiput is in the anterior position. The handle of the *left* blade held in the *left* hand is inserted to the *left* side of the pelvis in front of the child's *left* ear. The cardinal points shift to the right when dealing with the right blade. It is also important to remember that in all *left* sided positions of the occiput the *left* ear is posterior and in right sided positions the right ear is posterior. In posterior positions the posterior ear is on the opposite side of the pelvis from that of the corresponding anterior position. That is, in an L.O.P. position the left or posterior ear is on the right side.

With the sagittal suture in the perpendicular, the left blade is applied first. This facilitates locking the handles after application of the right blade since the lock is usually on the left. With the sagittal suture in the oblique diameter of the pelvis, the posterior blade (left blade for L.O.A. and right for R.O.A.) is applied first. By using the posterior blade technic, a splint is thus provided for the head tending to keep it in its anterior position, and preventing its backward rotation to the transverse or even posterior position during the application of the anterior blade. This advantage far outweighs the slight disadvantage of the necessity for crossing the handles to accomplish locking in the R.O.A. position.

Application for Left Occiput Anterior

In an L.O.A., the left ear is posterior. Therefore, the posterior blade is the left blade, the handle of which fits the operator's left hand and it is introduced to the left side of the pelvis, in front of the left ear.

After discarding temporarily the right blade, the operator stands with his back to the patient's right knee holding the handle of the blade in his left hand by the pencil grip. The pelvic curve of the blade is directed downward and the cephalic curve inward toward the vulva, with the plane of the shank perpendicular to the floor and parallel to the long axis of the patient. This position directs the blade properly on its intended course along the curved plane of the head and the left posterior side of the pelvis to its intended place in front of the left ear. Any other position of the blade starts it in the wrong direction, and necessitates rotation within the vulva to the cephalo-pelvic plane in order to avoid resistance. The middle and index fingers of the right hand are then inserted into the vagina opposite the posterior or left parietal bone to guide the toe of the blade along the side of the head. The right thumb is placed against the heel of the blade. The force necessary to carry the blade into the vagina to its proper place is applied here, not with the left hand at the handle. The left hand merely guides the handle downward over an arc, first outward toward the right thigh, then inward toward the mid-line as the blade enters the vagina (Fig. 13). Force applied at the handle may be uncontrolled and unconsciously increased if resistance is met, thereby causing damage. The force exerted by the thumb at the heel is limited, and since

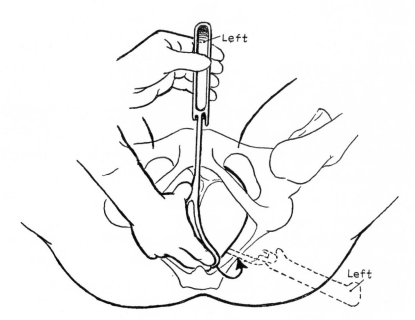

FIG. 13.   Introduction of left (posterior) blade for L.O.A.

it is applied directly on the blade is less likely to deflect it from its proper course. When the blade has been applied, if the pressure of the pelvis is not sufficient, an assistant holds it exactly as placed. In an L.O.A. position the plane of the handle should be parallel to the left oblique diameter of the pelvis, at right angles to the sagittal suture, or approximately coinciding with a line connecting ten and four on the dial of the clock.

The mistake often made by beginners is to change the handle so that it is parallel to the floor. This is an incorrect application unless the head has also rotated to the O.A. position with the sagittal suture perpendicular to the horizontal coinciding with a line connecting twelve and six on the dial of the clock.

In applying the second or anterior blade the four cardinal points shift from left to right and the operator changes his position so that his back is now opposite the patient's left knee. The right blade, held in the right hand, is applied similarly except that the toe is inserted anteriorly on the right side at a higher level so that it is adjacent to the anterior frontal bone. If inserted posteriorly as the left blade was, it has to be guided around the brow to the anterior or right ear by the middle and index fingers which have replaced the thumb at the heel of the blade. In doing this, the fenestration may catch on a corner of the brow causing the head to rotate back to an L.O.T. position. Thus, the good application of the first blade is lost. The result is often the undesirable brow-mastoid application.

When the right blade is in place the handles are locked

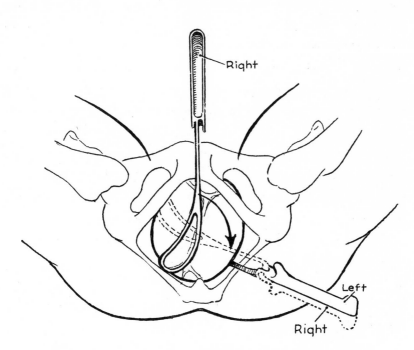

FIG. 14. Introduction of right (anterior) blade for
L.O.A. and locking of handles.

(Fig. 14). The left is not moved. Since it was applied first it is more apt to be in the correct position. The right is adjusted to fit it. If the handles do not lock easily or if they diverge widely when locked, the application is incorrect. Usually this is due to incomplete rotation of the anterior blade beyond the brow on the cheek and a short application. This is overcome by lowering of the handle after unlocking it and elevation of the blade by exerting upward pressure on the heel of the right blade with the middle and index fingers of the left hand, carrying it further up into the pelvis and around to the side of the head. If this maneuver is not successful, the forceps should be removed, the position of the head carefully checked, and if found to be the same, the procedure is repeated.

After the handles are locked satisfactorily, the application is checked. This is done in three ways:

First. The *posterior fontanelle* should be located, midway between the sides of the blades and one finger's breadth above the plane of the shanks.

Second. The *sagittal suture* should be perpendicular throughout its length to the plane of the shanks.

Third. The *fenestrations* of the blades should barely be felt if at all. Not more than the tip of a finger can be inserted between them and the head.

Unless these conditions are fulfilled the application is not a true cephalic or biparietal bimalar application. Readjustment of the blades is therefore necessary. This may be done without removing them. It is more easily accomplished after rotating the head counterclockwise with the forceps, without traction, until the sagittal suture is in the O.A. position. Attempts at readjustment before rotation of the occiput to anterior often result in upward displacement of the head, backward rotation to L.O.T., and no improvement in the application (Fig. 15).

Readjustment

If the posterior fontanelle is found to be more than one finger's breadth above the plane of the shanks, the correction is very easily made. The handles are unlocked and then elevated, one at a time, to the required level and relocked. If traction is applied without this correction the result is the same as traction on a deflexed head. The pivot point of the head is above the center of the blades. Traction causes the head to extend. This requires more force with the accompanying risk of injury to accomplish the delivery.

If the posterior fontanelle is less than a finger's breadth above or even below the plane of the shanks, the pivot point of the head is below the center of the blades. The application is in the overflexed attitude with the toes of the blades too far forward on the cheeks. Traction causes overflexion of the head. This correction is made by depressing or sinking the handles against the perineum one at a time, after unlocking them, until the shanks are at the desired level below the posterior fontanelle.

When the sagittal suture runs obliquely to the plane of the shanks it signifies a brow-mastoid application. Many of the milder degrees of this type of application are not recognized unless the examining finger is passed along the

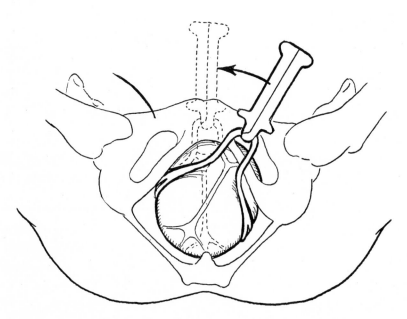

FIG. 15.   Rotation of L.O.A. with Simpson type forceps to
O.A. preliminary to traction.

entire length of the sagittal suture to determine its ultimate direction.

Correction is made by unlocking the handles and loosening one blade at a time, usually the posterior one first, without removal. The posterior or left blade is carried backward toward the posterior ear until the plane of the shank is at right angles with the sagittal suture and is then held in place by an assistant. The anterior or right blade is carried forward toward the anterior ear by depressing the handle and elevating the blade with the aid of the middle and index fingers of the left hand at the heel. After locking the handles the head is again rotated to the anterior position. Occasionally, the entire maneuver may have to be repeated if the result is not at first satisfactory.

In the third check of the application, if more than one-half inch of fenestration is felt below the head it is significant of a short application. The toe of the blade is not anchored well beyond the malar eminence. This is one cause of the forceps slipping during traction. If the operator is not prepared, the blades may come entirely off the head causing deep lacerations. In the correction the unlocked blades, one at a time, are carried up further into the pelvis until the fenestration cannot be felt below the head. The handles are then depressed and locked. After a final check of the application and anterior rotation, the next step is traction.

Application for Right Occiput Anterior

The technic of application for the R.O.A. is similar to that for the L.O.A. except that the order of applying the blades is reversed. The posterior blade in the R.O.A. position is the right blade and is applied first. It is held in the right hand and inserted posteriorly to the right side of the pelvis in front of the right ear (Fig. 16). Then the left blade, held in the left hand, is applied anteriorly to the left side of the pelvis in front of the left ear (Fig. 17). Since the standard lock is on the shank of the left blade, it will be necessary to separate the handles and cross the upper or left handle under that of the lower or right handle in order to lock them (Fig. 18). The Mount Reversed Lock eliminates the necessity for this maneuver in an R.O.A. position since the lock is constructed on the shank of the right blade. After clockwise rotation to the O.A. position (Fig. 19), checking the application, and making the necessary readjustments, traction is begun.

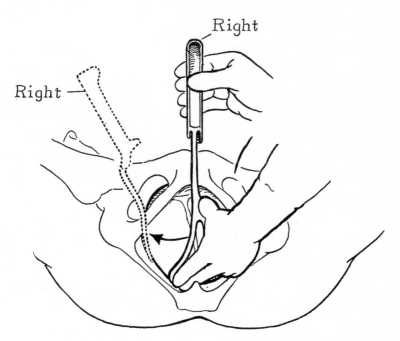

Right

Right

FIG. 16. Introduction of right (posterior) blade for R.O.A.

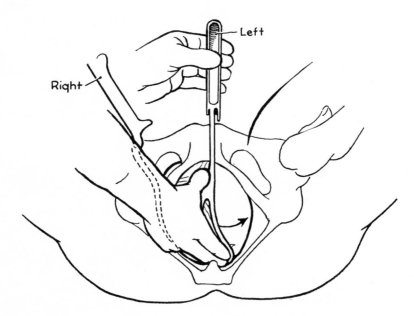

FIG. 17.   Introduction of left (anterior) blade for R.O.A.

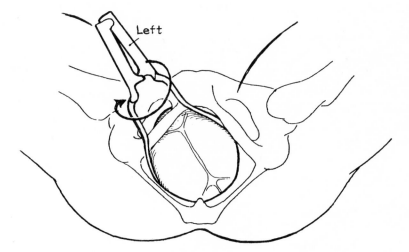

FIG. 18. Crossing handles (left under right)
for locking in R.O.A.

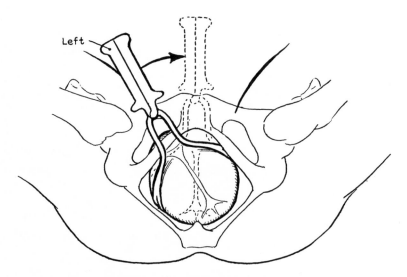

Fɪɢ. 19.   Rotation of R.O.A. with Simpson type forceps
to O.A. preliminary to traction.

CHAPTER 5

Traction

TRACTION should always be in the axis of the pelvis. A picture of the pelvic curve which is fishhook in shape, should be kept in mind at all times when making traction. Force is applied in a plane perpendicular to the plane of the pelvis at which the head is stationed. Therefore, the higher the head, the lower and more backward from the horizontal is the line of traction. As the head descends, the line of traction moves forward in a curved line following the curve of the sacrum. The pelvic curve of the classical instrument directs the handles in a plane obliquely anterior to the plane of the pelvis at which the head is stationed. Therefore, traction in the direction of the handles alone results in the force being wasted against the symphysis, with the accompanying injuries, and little or no advancement of the head (Fig. 20).

To apply the force in the plane of least resistance, that is, the axis of the pelvis, the axis-traction principle must be employed. This may be accomplished manually. One hand grasps the shanks and the other hand the handles. Force is

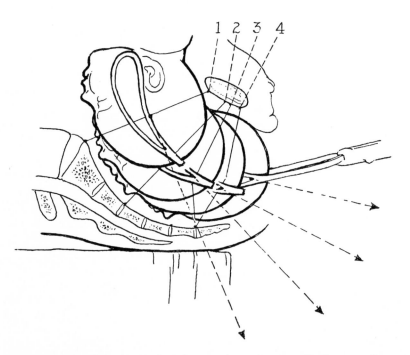

FIG. 20. Showing line of axis traction (perpendicular to the plane of the pelvis at which the head is stationed) at different planes of the pelvis. 1. High. 2. Mid. 3. Low-Mid. 4. Low.

exerted in two directions, downward with the hand on the shanks and outward with the hand on the handles, in a manner similar to the Pajot or Saxtorph Maneuvers (Fig. 21). This method is followed by varying degrees of success, depending upon the skill and strength of the operator and the station of the head. The higher the head, the more difficult it is to get axis traction by the manual method. Axis traction is *best* obtained with some form of axis-traction attachment to the forceps. The attachment either to the fenestrations, the shanks, the handles, or as in other types the backward bend of the shanks and handles, permits traction to be applied in a lower plane approaching that of the pelvic axis (Figs. 22, 23, 24, 25).

The axis-traction principle is desirable in any station of the head. Even in low forceps it is valuable in gaining flexion and eliminating force wasted against the symphysis. An episiotomy may allow the shanks to be depressed and lie in a lower plane. This, with the use of a hand on the shanks as a fulcrum, may eliminate the necessity of axis-traction forceps on low heads. However, the axis-traction attachment automatically directs force away from the symphysis into the plane of least resistance, thereby requiring the least expenditure of effort and minimizing injury to mother and child. Not all forceps have axis traction. This disadvantage can be overcome in those of the Elliot type with the Tiemann handle by the use of the Bill axis-traction handle which can be attached to the finger guards.

Traction may be applied from either the sitting or standing position. The sitting position is preferable, since axis

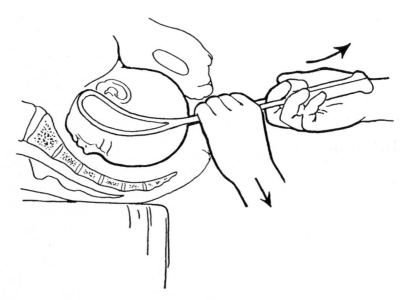

FIG. 21.   Manual method of axis traction —
Pajot-Saxtorph Maneuver.

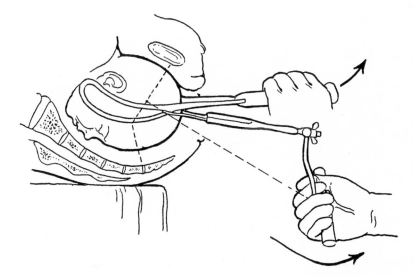

FIG. 22. Instrumental axis traction. (1) Irving.

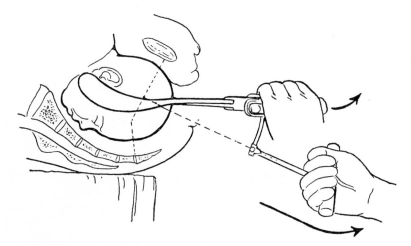

FIG. 23.   Instrumental axis traction.   (2) Tucker-McLane,
solid blades with Bill handle.

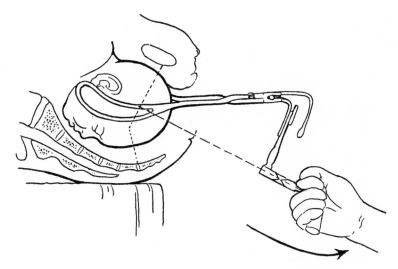

FIG. 24.   Instrumental axis traction.   (3) DeWees.

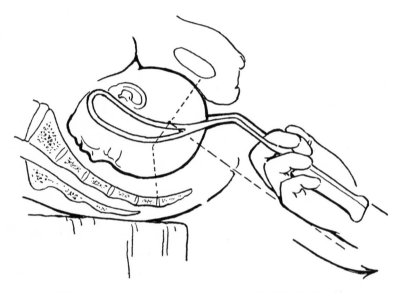

FIG. 25.   Instrumental axis traction.   (4) Hawks-Dennen.

traction is desired on every case and is best obtained in this way. The operator sits directly in front of the patient with his right foot behind him to extend his line of base and brace himself against sudden advancement of the head or slipping of the forceps. If the instrument has no axis-traction attachment, the handles rest in the upturned palm of the right hand. The shanks separate the middle and index fingers which grasp the fingerguards in the Elliot type of forceps. If a Simpson type is used, the middle finger occupies the space between the shanks and the adjacent fingers grasp the fingerguards. By holding the handles in this manner, a third degree lever action is attained, as the force of traction is applied at the lock and finger guards instead of at the handles. Thus compression of the fetal head from squeezing the handles is avoided.

The left hand grasps the shanks at the vulva from below. This provides a fulcrum for the forceps similar to the Saxtorph or Pajot Maneuvers. It is a movable fulcrum capable of exerting force downward in order to keep the head away from the symphysis, thus avoiding injury to the anterior wall of the vagina.

The right, or traction hand, applies traction outward in the direction of the handles and the left or fulcrum hand pulls directly toward the floor. The resultant of these two forces tends toward axis traction. As the head begins to distend the perineum, the direction of the pull changes to follow a curved plane forward and upward. This change in direction is carried out gradually and during traction only, following the plane of least resistance. The sense of resistance gradually becomes automatic as experience increases. If the direction of pull is changed too soon, resistance is met at the symphysis and subpubic angle; if too late, the coccyx and perineal floor offer resistance. The fulcrum hand is the guide to the axis of the pelvis. Its force is increased if resistance is met at the symphysis and diminished if the resistance is posterior.

Traction is made with a steady pull which is gradually increased in intensity, sustained for a definite interval and then gradually relaxed, simulating the character of a labor pain. The amount of force necessary for a gradual advance of the head and the number of tractions necessary for delivery vary with the type of case.* The pull is from the flexed forearms only, with elbows held close to the body. The operator is thus guarded against any sudden advance of the head or slipping of the blades. During the rest period between tractions, the handles may be unlocked and separated temporarily to relieve pressure on a loop of cord which may be caught by the toe of the blade. Auscultation of the fetal heart may help in anticipating this as well as other fetal complications.

If resistance is encountered at the outlet due to a short anteroposterior diameter or a prominent coccyx, the head is rotated back to the oblique diameter, either the L.O.A. or R.O.A. position depending upon which side the occiput was originally. After traction in this position has brought the

---

* The average amount of force exerted during traction reported by various investigators (Ullery et al., Fleming et al., Wylie, Pearce, etc.) varies between 34 and 45 pounds for the primapara and 24 to 29 pounds for the multipara.

head past the point of obstruction, the occiput is rotated forward to the O.A. position preliminary to extension.

When the posterior fontanelle has passed beyond the subpubic angle the head is ready for extension, except in cases of extreme molding. The legs are lowered almost to the horizontal to relieve tension on the perineum. At this time an episiotomy may be done. Some operators prefer to do it before applying the forceps, in order to avoid the possibility of early injury to soft parts during traction. Those who prefer doing the episiotomy in the later stage have the advantages of the rectum being pushed back out of the field by the head away from the scissors' points, and of less bleeding due to compression of the blood vessels in the distended perineum.

In extension of the head over the perineum, the handles are elevated by the left, or fulcrum hand, leaving the right, or traction hand, free to perform the modified Ritgen Maneuver. When the handles have been elevated to an angle of about forty-five degrees above the horizontal, the fingers of the right hand, protected by a sterile towel, catch the chin through the perineum behind the anus preventing the head from receding. The uncovered thumb of the same hand is placed directly against the occiput to prevent a precipitous advance of the head during the removal of the blades.

The blades are removed by a reversal of the motion used in applying them. The right blade is removed first. After unlocking, the handle of the right blade is carried over an arc toward the left groin and up to the symphysis. This is done with the left hand, as the right is occupied in the Ritgen Maneuver. As the handle is elevated, it is rotated so that the blade emerges from the vagina across the occiput in a curved plane with the cephalic curve of the blade following the curve of the head. At the completion of this maneuver the plane of the shank is perpendicular to the horizontal and parallel to the long axis of the patient (Fig. 26). The left blade is removed with the same hand in a similar manner toward the right side.

If resistance is encountered in removing the right blade, the left may be removed first. If both blades tend to stick, traction is not made on the handle because of the risk of injury to both the mother and the child from forcible extraction. It is better to place the thumb of the right hand, resting on the occiput, inside the fenestration of the right blade, then guide the blade out around the head with pressure on the inner edge of the posterior lip of the fenestration. For the left blade, this gentle extraction maneuver is carried out in the opposite direction with the untowelled right index finger. If too much resistance is encountered in removing the blades, it is advisable to deliver the head with one or both blades *in situ*.

If an axis-traction attachment to the forceps is used much less effort will be necessary for the delivery, since the force is automatically directed in the axis of the pelvis. The higher the head, the more imperative is this principle. Also the higher the head, the lower should be the stool on which the operator sits. Thus, traction in the proper plane is favored. The height of the stool for most low and low-mid forceps should be such as to have the operator sitting "chin high" to the patient's symphysis. When using an instrument with an

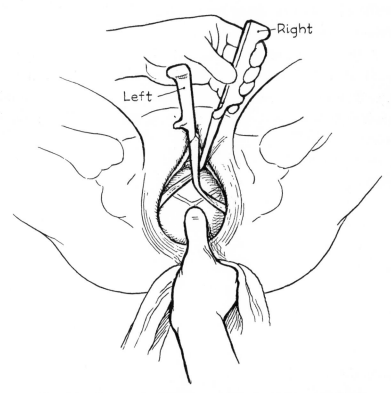

Fɪɢ. 26.   Removal of forceps while head is controlled
by the modified Ritgen Maneuver.

axis-traction attachment, the right hand, palm up, applies force to the traction bar in a direction perpendicular to the plane of the pelvis at which the head is arrested. Some axis-traction attachments have an indicator to show the proper direction. The left hand on the handles directs the course of the descending head.

After removal of the forceps, the head is delivered by the modified Ritgen Maneuver. Restitution is completed manually. The legs are re-elevated to the lithotomy position and the shoulders and body of the child are delivered in the usual manner.

CHAPTER 6

Transverse Positions of the Occiput

IN THE L.O.T. position it is often difficult to get a good application with the classical instrument. It is even more difficult in the R.O.T. position, because the handles must be crossed to lock them and an accurate application may be lost by this maneuver. Before applying the blades, the operator may choose to rotate the head digitally or manually to the anterior position.

Digital and Manual Rotation — Left Occiput Transverse

The hand used in the rotation depends upon the position of the head. In left-sided positions rotation is accomplished with the right hand, since that is the hand used later to guide the introduction of the posterior or left blade. With the left hand making counter pressure on the fundus, the vagina is ironed out. Then after checking the position, the digital rotation maneuver is used. If successful, the more complicated manual rotation maneuver is unnecessary. In digital

69

rotation, the tips of the index and middle fingers of the right hand are placed in the anterior segment of the lambdoidal suture near the posterior fontanelle. The elevated edge of the anterior parietal bone, bounded by this suture offers resistance to the hooked fingertips so that, when a lifting motion is carried out, the occiput may be turned in a counter-clockwise direction to the L.O.A. or even the O.A. position. Counter pressure with the fundal hand tends to fix the head in the new position. Without removal, the two rotating fingers are slipped behind the posterior parietal bone to prevent backward rotation of the occiput and act as a guide to the introduction of the left (posterior) blade.

If digital rotation is unsuccessful, the manual maneuver is used. The four fingers of the right hand are introduced into the vagina behind the posterior parietal bone with the palm up and the thumb over the anterior parietal bone. The head is grasped with the tips of the fingers and thumb. If the entire hand is introduced into the vagina, the head may be displaced or even disengaged. This should be avoided, since the higher the head, the harder and more dangerous will be the operation. The head is flexed and rotated in a counter-clockwise direction to the anterior position (Fig. 27). Simultaneously, the left hand, placed on the abdomen, pulls the back of the child toward the midline. When this has been accomplished, pressure is made on the fundus to fix the head in the new position. In order to prevent the head from rotating back to its original position, only the thumb of the right hand is removed from the vagina, leaving the four fingers in place to splint the head and guide the introduction of the

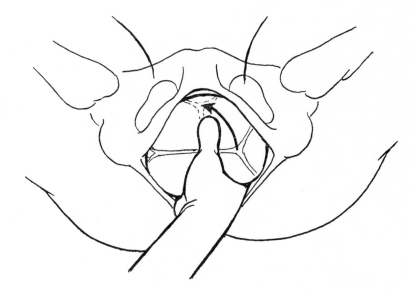

FIG. 27. Manual rotation from L.O.T. to anterior.

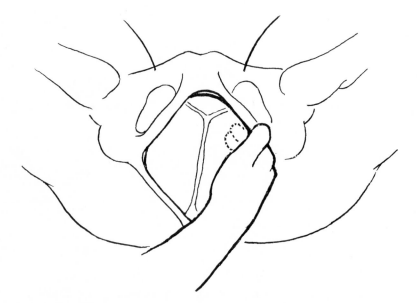

FIG. 28. I..O.A. after manual rotation from L.O.T.
Fingers of right hand in place, preventing backward
rotation of the head. Thumb is removed in prepara-
tion for introduction of posterior or left blade.

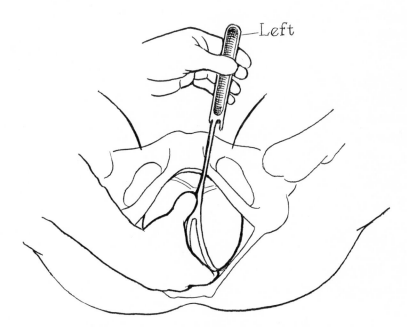

—Left

FIG. 29.   Insertion of left blade (Simpson type) to L.O.A.
after manual rotation from L.O.T.

left blade in the usual manner (Figs. 28 and 29). After the left blade has been applied, an assistant holds the handle firmly, exerting a slight amount of force in the direction of the patient's left leg. This presses the toe of the blade against the baby's left cheek and keeps the head in the anterior position. The right blade is introduced in the usual manner. This blade must be introduced high above the posterior frontal eminence to avoid this obstruction. The handle is carried to the right of the midline toward the patient's left thigh to throw the toe away from the obstructing anterior frontal eminence. Then the blade is lifted with the middle and index fingers of the left hand which have replaced the thumb at the heel, in order to bring it over the anterior parietal bone. If the fenestration catches on the frontal eminence, the head will rotate back to the L.O.T. position and the result will be a brow-mastoid application. After locking the shanks, the application is checked. If the head is in the L.O.A. position, rotation to the anteroposterior (O.A.) diameter is completed and the necessary readjustments are made before traction is started. If the application is unsatisfactory after two attempts at readjustment, both blades are removed, the position is checked, and the procedure is repeated.

Digital and Manual Rotation — Right Occiput Transverse

In this position the rotating and splinting hand is the left one. The right or posterior blade is held in the right hand and inserted to the right side of the pelvis over the right ear. The left or anterior blade held in the left hand is introduced high on the left side of the pelvis opposite the left ear in a similar manner as was the anterior blade in the L.O.T. position. The handles must be crossed in order to lock them, since the lock is on the left shank. The head, if in the R.O.A. position, is rotated without traction to the anteroposterior diameter, the application is checked, the necessary readjustments made, and traction and delivery are carried out in the usual manner.

In general the station of the head is an indication for the choice of the digital or the manual maneuver. With the head at low-mid station the digital maneuver is chosen because there is insufficient room between the head and the perineum for the manual maneuver without displacement of the head.

When the head is at mid station the digital maneuver is less likely to be successful and there is room to insert the hand for the manual maneuver without the necessity of the initial displacement.

Instrumental Rotation — Left Occiput Transverse

An accurate application of forceps to the head in the transverse position is more difficult to accomplish than in the oblique position, because the anterior blade has to be carried or "wandered" over a longer arc around the face to the anterior ear directly under the symphysis. In doing this, more points of obstruction may be met. When a proper application is accomplished, the plane of the shanks is directed toward the side on which the occiput lies, obliquely away from the midline of the long axis of the patient at an angle of about fifty degrees. The amount of deviation depends upon the degree of the pelvic curve of the forceps.

The left blade is introduced first, directly posterior instead of to the left side of the patient. Therefore, the approach differs from that of the anterior position in that the plane of the shank is not perpendicular to the horizontal, but runs obliquely to it, in order to allow for the pelvic curve of the blade. The toe of the blade is directly posterior and the blade follows the parallel to the plane of the sacrum with the shank following obliquely to the plane of the sacrum. The blade hugs the head to avoid obstruction. As the blade enters the vagina, the handle is lowered until it reaches a point just below the horizontal, or until the fenestration can barely be felt below the head. The angle the handle makes with the horizontal will depend upon the station of the head. "The higher the head, the lower the handle" (Fig. 30).

The right blade is held in the right hand and introduced to the right side of the pelvis high up under the ramus, since the brow is more anterior than in the L.O.A., due to its transverse position (Fig. 31). The handle is then made to descend over an arc close to the left thigh until it comes to rest directly below the handle of the left blade. This maneuver throws the toe of the blade away from the anterior frontal eminence into a position from which it can be wandered around the head into place, just in front of the anterior ear, by an upward lift of the middle finger of the left hand placed at the heel (Fig. 32). As the handle of the wandering blade approaches the handle of the posterior or left blade it will be found to be in a lower plane. In order to lock them it will be necessary to

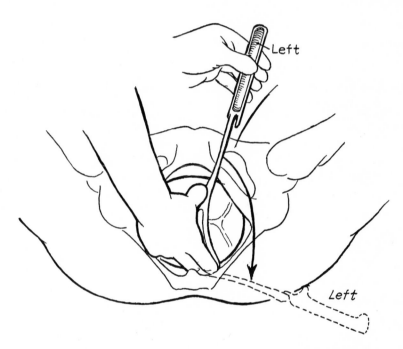

Fig. 30. Introduction of posterior or left blade (Elliot) for instrumental rotation of L.O.T. to O.A.

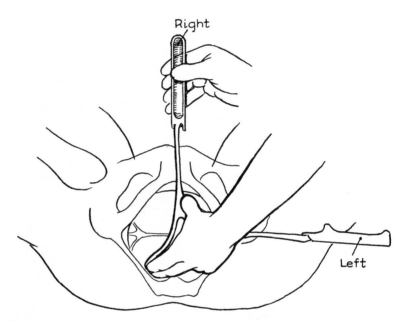

FIG. 31.   Introduction of anterior or right blade (Elliot)
for instrumental rotation of L.O.T. to O.A.

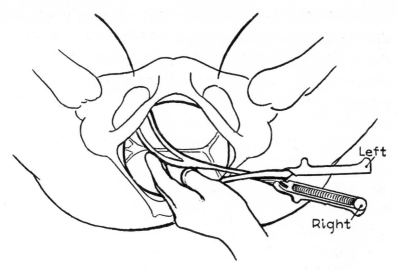

FIG. 32. Wandering maneuver of anterior or right blade of Elliot forceps in application to L.O.T.

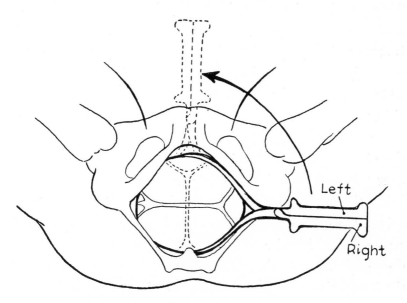

FIG. 33. Instrumental rotation of L.O.T. to O.A.

elevate the handle of the right blade, causing the blade to slide further up into the pelvis behind the symphysis until the handles meet. When locked, the handles lie in a plane obliquely to the left of the midline of the patient. This is necessary in order to bring the plane of the shanks one finger's breadth mediad to the posterior fontanelle.

The steps in instrumental rotation of the head are: compression of the handles, flexion and rotation over an arc, and depression of the handles. After checking the application, counterclockwise rotation of the handles is made over a wide arc to the anterior position (Fig. 33). Flexion is important and should be done during rotation. The handles are squeezed tightly to prevent the blades from riding on the face. They are then carried toward the midline to promote flexion and at the same time rotated counterclockwise over an arc of about ninety degrees until the posterior fontanelle is under the symphysis. If the head will not rotate, it is probably because the handles are not being rotated over a wide arc, or the head is extended, or the head is arrested either at, or near, the plane of the inlet or at the plane of the ischial spines. The plane of choice for rotation is midpelvis, the plane of greatest pelvic dimension. If the arrest is at or near the inlet, traction is made before rotation in order to bring the head to midpelvis. If the arrest is at the ischial spines, the head is pushed up slightly so that rotation can be accomplished in midpelvis. Rotation is over an arc, because the pelvic curve of the blades directs the handles away from the long axis of the patient. During the completion of rotation the handles are depressed to preserve or improve flexion. The application is again checked and the blades are readjusted if necessary. Traction is made in the axis of the pelvis.

Instrumental Rotation — Right Occiput Transverse

In R.O.T. positions the right or posterior blade is introduced first. This is done by holding the right blade in the right hand and applying it directly posterior to the right ear. The force exerted to introduce the blade is made by the thumb pressing against the heel. The handle descends toward the right thigh so that the shank will be one finger's breadth mediad to the posterior fontanelle. This avoids an application in the extended attitude. The handle may be held in this position by an assistant while the left blade is introduced high on the left side and wandered anteriorly in the usual manner. In right-sided positions the handles must be crossed in order to lock them. In doing this, the finger guard may interfere with the crossing. Therefore, one handle is pulled down while the other handle is pushed up. Then the crossing is facilitated. A preliminary check of the application is made, and if found to be either good or fair, the head is flexed and rotated by carrying the handles clockwise over an arc to the anterior position. The application is rechecked; readjustments which are so frequently found necessary in this position are made, and extraction is completed in the usual manner. If the application is not satisfactory after attempts at readjustment, the blades are removed and, after checking the position, are reapplied. Traction is always in the axis of the pelvis and is best accomplished with some form of axis-traction instrument.

The wandering maneuver of applying the anterior blade to the transverse head is more easily accomplished with the Elliot type of blade, because of its round, cephalic curve which offers less resistance than the Simpson while passing under the symphysis. Also the overlapping shanks offer less resistance to rotation.

CHAPTER 7

Posterior Positions of the Occiput

POSTERIOR POSITIONS are handled either by manual rotation or instrumental rotation to the anterior position, or by a combination of these two methods. Only in very rare instances is the head delivered as a posterior.

Manual Rotation — L.O.P. and R.O.P.

Manual rotation of a posterior head is accomplished in the same manner as is the transverse head with the exception that the head must be rotated over a longer arc to the anterior position. The right hand is the rotating hand for an L.O.P. (Fig. 34), and the left for an R.O.P. After rotation to an anterior quadrant of the pelvis is accomplished manually, the thumb of the rotating hand is removed from the vagina while pressure is made on the fundus by the assistant. The four fingers remain in place behind the posterior parietal bone in order to splint the head and prevent it from rotating back to the transverse or posterior position while the posterior blade is being applied. The posterior blade in left-sided position

83

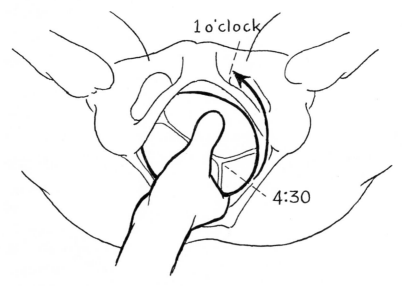

F<small>IG</small>. 34.   Manual rotation of L.O.P. to anterior with right hand.

of the occiput is the left blade. Its handle is held in the left hand and it is inserted on the left side of the pelvis opposite the left ear. In right-sided positions it is the right blade with the right hand at the handle. After the posterior blade has been placed in position opposite the posterior ear, the fingers of the rotating hand are removed from the vagina so that they can hold the handle of the anterior blade. This is introduced in the usual manner for an anterior position. Then the shanks are locked, the application checked, rotation to O.A. is completed, the application is rechecked and the necessary readjustments are made before extraction is begun.

Manual Rotation — Pomeroy Maneuver

The object of the Pomeroy Maneuver is to change the position from the posterior to the opposite anterior position. Therefore, an L.O.P. is rotated manually to an R.O.A. and in complicated, stubborn cases the shoulders are manually changed to the opposite side of the mother's abdomen. By manually changing the shoulders, when they do not follow the head spontaneously, the rotation of the head can be completed and it will be held in the new anterior position. This maneuver may be accomplished before complete dilatation of the cervix, thereby shortening the first stage of labor which is being prolonged on account of the posterior position of the head, and reducing the tendency to abnormal contraction ring formation. The operator with a small hand has an advantage in performing this maneuver. Rotation is done under deep anesthesia. The disadvantage of this maneuver is the displacement of the head with the possible prolapse of the cord.

In left-sided positions the operator kneels with his back to the patient and inserts his left hand, palm down, with the fingers anterior to the head and the thumb posterior. The head is pushed out of the pelvis and the anterior shoulder is grasped between the tips of the first and second fingers. Rotation is counterclockwise in the L.O.P. position and is continued 180 degrees until the occiput comes to the R.O.A. position.

Resistance to complete rotation may be overcome by simultaneously rotating the anterior shoulder with the fingers which grasp it. At the same time, the assistant aids the rotation by exerting abdominal pressure on the baby's back toward and beyond the midline. As the rotation is being completed the operator rises and faces the patient. Pressure is applied to the fundus and suprapubic region to fix the head in the pelvis. If dilatation is complete and the head comes down well into the pelvis, it may be delivered by forceps when indicated. If dilatation is incomplete the patient is allowed to come out of anesthesia and continue in labor to be delivered subsequently either spontaneously or instrumentally (Fig. 35).

In right-sided positions the head is rotated with the right hand in a clockwise direction 180 degrees from R.O.P. to L.O.A. Cochran advised spinal anesthesia for the rotation to avoid repeating the general anesthesia if the delivery is postponed.

In this form of dystocial labor, modern methods of management, such as use of analgesia, oxytoxic stimulation, the Kielland forceps, and the vacuum extractor, have outmoded this maneuver.

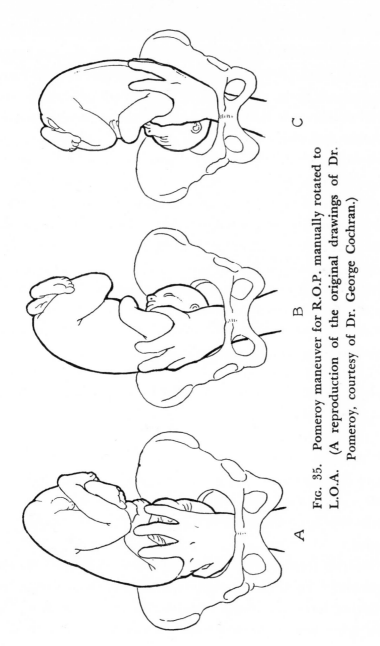

Fig. 35. Pomeroy maneuver for R.O.P. manually rotated to L.O.A. (A reproduction of the original drawings of Dr. Pomeroy, courtesy of Dr. George Cochran.)

Combined Manual and Instrumental Rotation

If rotation of a posterior head cannot be accomplished manually beyond the transverse position it may be completed instrumentally by applying the forceps as in a transverse arrest as described by Williamson. The rotating hand is kept in place to act as a splint while the posterior blade is being applied (Fig. 36). The anterior blade is wandered around the brow by the elevating fingers at the heel, as the handle is depressed well below the handle of the posterior blade. When the blade is in place behind the symphysis opposite the anterior ear, the handle is elevated to the locking position beneath the handle of the posterior blade. The completion of the rotation of the head instrumentally to the O.A. position is in a counter-clockwise direction for left-sided positions. In right-sided positions the direction is clockwise. After checking the application traction is applied.

Instrumental Rotation — Modified Scanzoni Maneuver — L.O.P.

The modified Scanzoni maneuver consists in complete instrumental rotation, with the Elliot type of forceps, of an occiput posterior to the anterior position. It is accomplished with a single maneuver but requires a double application of the forceps for completion of the delivery.

An L.O.P. is considered as an R.O.A. and the blades are applied accordingly. Therefore, in the L.O.P. position the right blade, held in the right hand, is applied first over the left or posterior ear in the right side of the pelvis (Fig. 37). This is the first deviation from the cardinal point of the left

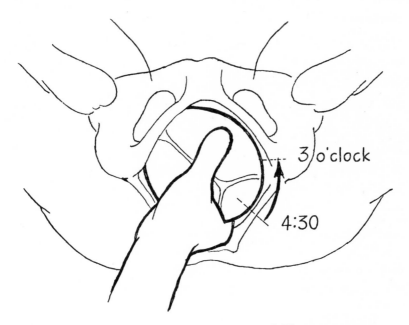

Fig. 36. Manual rotation of L.O.P. to L.O.T. preparatory to application of Elliot type of forceps to L.O.T. using the wandering method for the anterior blade and completion of rotation to O.A. instrumentally.

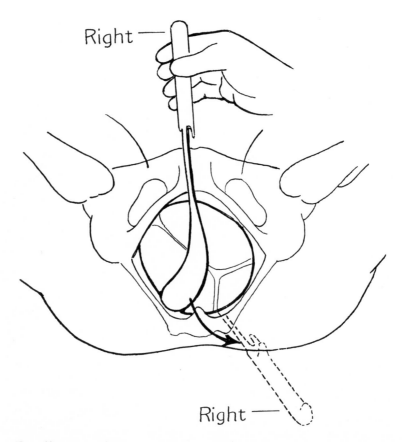

FIG. 37. Insertion of posterior or right blade (Tucker-McLane), solid Elliot type in the first stage of the modified Scanzoni maneuver for instrumental rotation of L.O.P. to O.A.

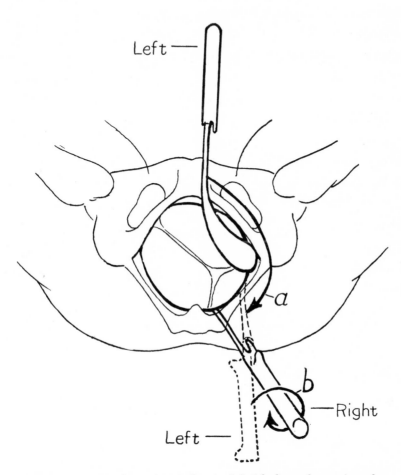

FIG. 38. Insertion of anterior or left blade and crossing the handle, left over right, for locking in the first stage of the modified Scanzoni maneuver for L.O.P.

blade to the left ear. After the right blade is applied, the left blade is taken in the left hand and applied to the left side of the pelvis to the child's right or anterior ear. The handles are crossed and the shanks locked (Fig. 38). A preliminary check should show the posterior fontanelle to be just *below* the plane of the shanks and the sagittal suture perpendicular to the plane of the shanks. The head is then rotated counter-clockwise to the anterior position. The pelvic curve of the forceps makes it necessary to rotate the handles over a wide arc to keep the blades in the center of the pelvis, thereby avoiding obstruction or injury. Frequently, the head is extended. Therefore, if flexion is performed first, rotation will be made much easier because the resistance will be decreased. If the widest part of the head is arrested at the plane of the ischial spines, it will be necessary to push it up 1 or 2 cm. to loosen it and to bring it into the greatest pelvic diameter. If the head is arrested near the plane of the inlet it will be necessary to pull it down to mid-pelvis before rotating.

In L.O.P. positions, rotation is counter-clockwise. After the handles are elevated in order to procure flexion, and after they are rotated in order to bring the occiput into the anterior oblique (L.O.A.) diameter of the pelvis, the head is fixed in the new position by one downward traction. Since the blades are now upside down with the toes pointing posteriorly, they must be removed, reinverted, and reapplied (Fig. 39). The posterior (right) blade, which is the one over the left ear, is temporarily retained in place to splint the head in the anterior position. The anterior blade is removed first in a

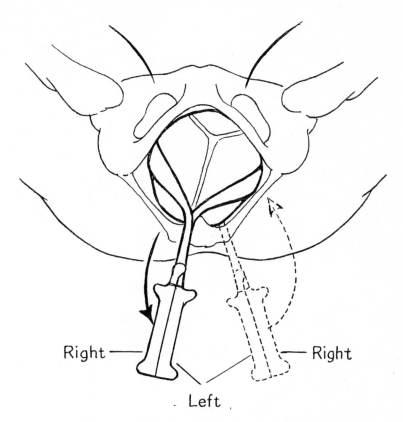

Right — — Right

Left

Fig. 39. Instrumental rotation, counterclockwise, from L.O.P. to anterior. This completes the first stage of the modified Scanzoni maneuver. The occiput is now anterior, but the blades are upside down. The second stage involves removal, reinversion, and reapplication.

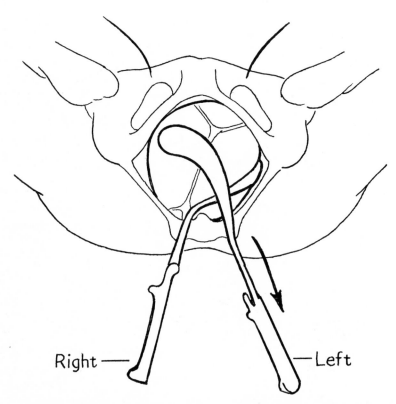

FIG. 40. Removal of the left or anterior blade downward, after one fixing pull in this direction.

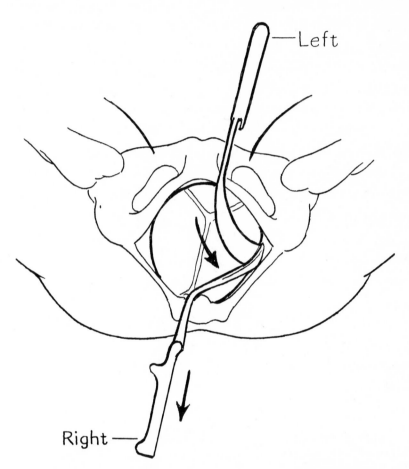

FIG. 41. Reinversion and reinsertion of the left blade between the splinting right blade and the posterior or left ear as for L.O.A.

downward direction (Fig. 40). Since it is the left blade, it is reinserted this time between the child's head and the blade which is still in place opposite the left ear, as in the L.O.A. technic (Fig. 41). Following this, the right, or "splinting" blade, is removed in a downward direction and reapplied over the right, or anterior ear (Fig. 42). In the original Scanzoni maneuver, after the head has been rotated to the anterior quadrant of the pelvis, both blades are removed without leaving the posterior one in place as a splint, and reapplied for the new anterior position. As a result, the head frequently rotates back toward the original position before the reapplication can be made.

In doing this modified Scanzoni maneuver it has been found that the Elliot type of forceps with overlapping shanks, especially the Tucker-McLane with solid blades or the Luikart modification, offers less resistance to application and removal and causes less injury during rotation of the head. Also, the Bill axis-traction handle is an aid to rotation as well as to traction. A fenestrated Simpson type of blade may be used for the second application and traction in a similar manner as the "two forceps maneuver" described by Seides. It is very easy to slip a fenestrated blade between the child's head and the posterior splinting solid blade. The solid blade obviates the possibility of threading the first reapplied blade through the fenestration of the splinting blade. If this should happen, it complicates the removal of the splinting blade. However, the removal can be facilitated by withdrawing the blade along the surrounded shank past the finger guard to the end of the handle.

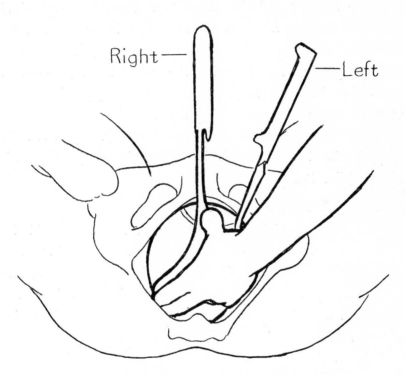

FIG. 42. Reapplication of the right splinting blade to the anterior right ear as in L.O.A., after removal in a downward direction and reinversion.

It is felt that the modified Scanzoni maneuver is preferable to the original maneuver, in that the head is less likely to slip back to the transverse or posterior position owing to the presence of the "splinting blade." It must be emphasized that after rotation of the head to the anterior position in the first stage of this maneuver the blades are upside down so that the pelvic curve is facing the pelvic floor. Therefore, removal of the blades must be accomplished by pulling downward on the handles toward the floor.

After the head has been rotated to the O.A. position the reapplication is checked and if found satisfactory, traction is begun (Fig. 43).

Scanzoni Maneuver — R.O.P.

The R.O.P. position is considered as an L.O.A., the blades applied and the head rotated clockwise to the anterior quadrant. Removal and reapplication is similar to that of the L.O.P., except that in the second application, that is, to the new R.O.A. position, the handles must be crossed in order to lock them.

The Jacobs forceps, an Elliot type, with solid blades attached to the shanks by a swivel joint, the La Breck forceps, a Simpson type with solid blades and swivel jointed toes, the Mann forceps, a Simpson type with a split universal joint, and the Miseo, an Elliot type with a split universal joint and parallel shanks, eliminate the necessity of removal and reapplication after rotation to anterior.

Instrumental Rotation — Key in Lock Maneuver

The DeLee "Key in Lock" maneuver is a gradual instrumental rotation of an occiput posterior to the anterior position by multiple readjustments of the forceps. The method

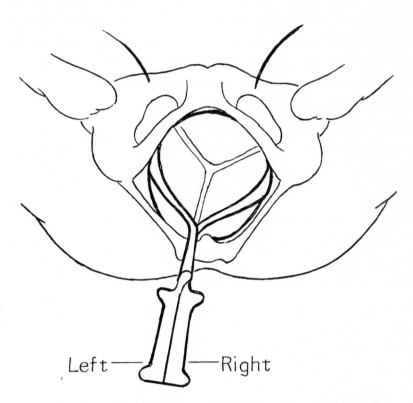

FIG. 43. The forceps are now properly applied and locked in the new L.O.A. position, ready for traction after completing rotation to O.A. The Bill handle should be added for traction.

tends to minimize injuries to the vagina which may occur following complete rotation with a single maneuver such as the Scanzoni. Injuries are more apt to occur if the single maneuver complete rotation is done with a Simpson type of forceps. The separated shanks and wide space between the heels tend to fill the pelvis and meet more points of resistance during rotation than do the Elliot type. Therefore, if a Simpson type, such as the DeLee forceps, is used for instrumental rotation the "Key in Lock" maneuver is adapted to it.

L.O.P.

In the L.O.P. position, the head is considered to be an R.O.A. and the blades applied for such a position. The head is pushed up 1 cm., flexed and rotated counterclockwise through an arc of five degrees and then pulled down. The handles are unlocked and the blades readjusted to the R.O.A. oblique. The handles are relocked, the head pushed up again 1 cm., flexed, rotated five degrees more, and pulled down. When the head has reached the L.O.T. position the blades are in the R.O.A. oblique with the brow-mastoid application. After the next readjustment the blades are changed to the L.O.A. oblique with the opposite brow-mastoid application. Care must be taken not to injure the anterior wall while moving the anterior blade under the pubic arch. Repeated readjustments eventually bring the head to the O.A. position with an O.A. application ready for traction.

R.O.P.

In the R.O.P. position the maneuver is begun by applying the blades as in an L.O.A. The rotation is clockwise (Fig. 44).

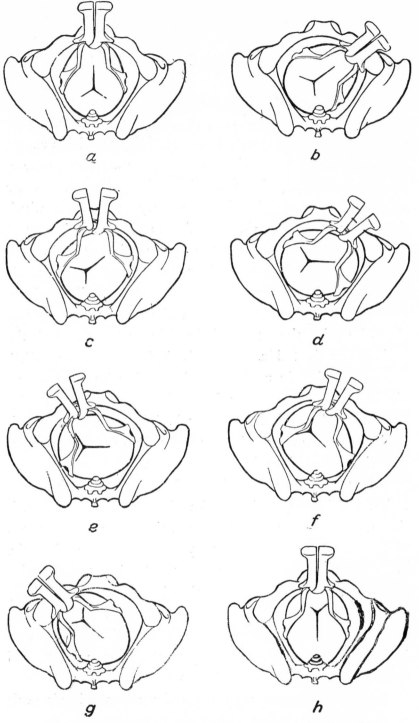

FIG. 44. Successive stages of the DeLee "key-in-lock" maneuver, for anterior rotation of an R.O.P. (A reproduction of Dr. DeLee's drawing in Surgery, Gynecology and Obstetrics, May 1928.)

Directly Posterior Heads (O.P.)

The occiput in the direct posterior position is treated the same as in the transverse or posterior oblique position except that it is rotated over a longer arc to the anterior position. The rotation may be manual or instrumental. Before attempting such rotation it is necessary to know on which side the child's back lies in order to know which way to rotate the head. This avoids the danger of injury to the neck from rotation in the wrong direction. The occiput normally points toward the side on which the child's back lies. Therefore, with the back to the left, the rotation is counterclockwise using the same technic as in an L.O.P. With the back on the right side, rotation is clockwise as in an R.O.P.

Occasionally, in an anthropoid pelvis with a transverse diameter too narrow to permit anterior rotation, the posterior occiput should be delivered as such. The same procedure is used in a case of a marked funnel pelvis with the occiput posterior molded into the outlet under a narrow arch.

The technic of application of forceps to an occiput posterior, which is to be delivered without anterior rotation, is similar to that for the first stage of the Scanzoni maneuver. Before locking the handles they are depressed against the perineum until the shanks are at the level of the posterior fontanelle. More effort in traction is necessary for delivery of an occiput posterior as such. After the anterior fontanelle appears under the symphysis, the head is delivered by flexion instead of by extension. Injury to the rectum is guarded against by a deep oblique episiotomy.

This discussion of posterior and transverse heads deals

only with the utilization of the classical instruments. Many cases are handled much more efficiently with less manipulation and less effort if the operator uses a special instrument, such as the Kielland or Barton forceps (see Chapters 8 and 10) and the more recently developed Laufe forceps.

Laufe Forceps

The Laufe forceps is a beautifully constructed instrument with an ingenious locking device for a hinged blade on one branch of the forceps. It should be quite effective, especially as a rotator, for the simpler cases of transverse and posterior arrest.

It combines in one instrument certain advantageous features of both the Kielland and the Barton forceps. However, in eliminating other features of each, which are disadvantages under certain conditions but are advantages under others, it creates disadvantages of its own, especially when used on the more complicated cases.

Lack of the backward curve, in the Laufe forceps, eliminates not only the most important advantage of the Kielland—an accurate application with the least amount of manipulation by the inversion method—but also the built-in principle of axis traction.

Elimination of the lateral curve attachment of the blades to the shanks in the Barton forceps does away with its most important advantage over other forceps. In a pelvis with a straight or deformed sacrum, this lateral curve permits the best line of traction on a head in the transverse position for descent before anterior rotation.

The features of construction are essential when selecting the instrument best suited for the individual case. Under special conditions the instrument, not infrequently, has made the difference between success and failure.

Operative Management of Occiput Posterior Positions

1. MANUAL ROTATION to occiput anterior
   A. Digital rotation
   B. Manual rotation } Followed by Simpson type forceps
   C. Pomeroy maneuver } (Hawks-Dennen Forceps)

2. COMBINED MANUAL AND INSTRUMENTAL ROTATION to occiput anterior

Wandering maneuver, Elliot type forceps after manual or digital rotation to transverse.

3. INSTRUMENTAL ROTATION to occiput anterior

A. Classical instrument

   a. Scanzoni maneuver (modified)
      Elliot type forceps (solid blade—Tucker-McLane) (Luikart)

   b. DeLee, Key-in-Lock maneuver
      Simpson type forceps

B. Modified Classical Instrument

   a. Jacobs-Elliot type, solid blade

   b. LaBreck-Simpson type, solid blade

   c. Mann-Simpson type, split universal joint

   d. Miseo-Elliot type, split universal joint (parallel shanks)

C. Special Instruments

   a. Kielland

   b. Barton

   c. Laufe

4. DELIVER AS A POSTERIOR POSITION

A. Android pelvis (selected cases) (Simpson type)
B. Anthropoid pelvis (selected cases) (Simpson type)

5. INTERNAL PODALIC VERSION

Piper forceps to after-coming head if delay.

CHAPTER 8

Special Instruments

KIELLAND FORCEPS

In 1915 Christian Kielland of Norway presented his forceps to the obstetrical world. Although originally intended for application to heads in deep transverse arrest this instrument is now used on posterior heads, face and brow presentations, and in some cases it is supplanting the cranioclast. It has been considered good for heads arrested at the inlet but that was not Kielland's original intention. Although this operation is rarely indicated, the Kielland is better than the average classical instrument for high forceps since it permits a more accurate application. It is now used almost exclusively by some obstetricians on occiputs not in one of the anterior quadrants of the pelvis.

Construction

This forceps has a slight pelvic curve which is backward, giving the instrument a bayonet shape. It has overlapping shanks with an extra long distance between the heels of the blades and the intersecting point of the shanks. The lock is a sliding one and is designed to care for asynclitism. The inner surface of the blades is beveled in order to prevent injury to the child's head. The knobs on each anterior surface of the finger guards are used to identify the anterior surface of the instrument and serve as a guide in the technic of application.

Advantages

A single accurate application without displacement of the head can be obtained by the inversion method because of the reverse pelvic curve.

The sliding lock principle permits adjustment of asynclitic heads and allows the locking of the handles at any level on the shank.

There is a semi axis-traction pull due to the reverse pelvic curve.

The beveled inner surface of the blades minimizes facial injury.

The extra long distance between the heels of the blades and the intersecting point of the shanks, lengthens the posterior portion of the cephalic curve of the instrument. This accommodates heads of different shapes and sizes regardless of molding.

Disadvantages

In a flat pelvis with a high transverse arrest of a posterior parietal presentation, the Kielland forceps are distinctly contraindicated. When applied to this position there is no available pelvic curve nor axis traction. The mechanism of a flat pelvis requires descent of the head in the transverse diameter until it reaches the plane of greatest pelvic dimension. Traction brings the bulge of the anterior blade against the symphysis endangering it and the bladder. A straight or forward jutting upper sacrum carries the same disadvantages regardless of the station of the head in transverse arrest. The head must be drawn well past the point of deformity, in the transverse position, before it can be rotated to anterior.

In a male type pelvis with a funnel outlet and a low symphysis, the reverse pelvic curve may cause injury to the posterior vaginal wall and perineum during extension. Also, during the same maneuver, elevation of the handles may bring that portion of the forceps connecting the blades with the shanks in contact with the pubic rami. The result may be a periostitis. Some operators prefer to remove the Kielland forceps after rotation and descent have been accomplished, substituting a suitable classical type of instrument with a good pelvic curve for extension.

Although this instrument has marked a great advance in obstetrical surgery, it is not a panacea. It is dangerous if not properly used. The accidents which may happen with its misuse are perforation of the uterus, separation of the symphysis, vesicovaginal fistula, perforation of the cul de sac, cervical and sulcus tears, and third degree laceration. However, all of these injuries may follow the use of any instrument. Many of them are seen in spontaneous deliveries. The fault is not so much with the instrument as with the manner of its use.

Kielland Technic

L.O.T. Position — Deep Transverse Arrest

Application—Inversion Method

Since the Kielland is a special type of instrument, the technic for the classical instrument of applying the posterior blade first is abandoned. Instead, the anterior blade is always applied first, preferably by the inversion method. In left-sided positions the left ear is posterior with the right ear anterior. This requires the application of the right blade first. The blades are locked and held outside the pelvis, directed toward the patient in a position similar to that which they will assume when applied (Fig. 45). The knobs will be pointing in the direction of the occiput, toward the patient's left leg at 3 o'clock. The anterior blade is easily distinguished as the one on top, and it is found to be the right blade since there is no lock on its shank. This blade, after temporarily discarding the left blade, is held in an inverted manner with the inner surface of the cephalic curve facing upward and the shank forty-five degrees above the horizontal.

The blade, the handle of which is held in the right hand, rests in the palm of the left hand, the tips of the middle and index fingers of which are inserted under the symphysis anterior to the head in search of the anterior lip of the cervix (Fig. 46). The toe is passed directly under the symphysis and is guided inside the cervix, if present, by the finger tips. If the cervix cannot be felt, the toe, when it has passed the finger tips, is kept close to the head until the fenestration has disappeared from sight. By this time the handle has been

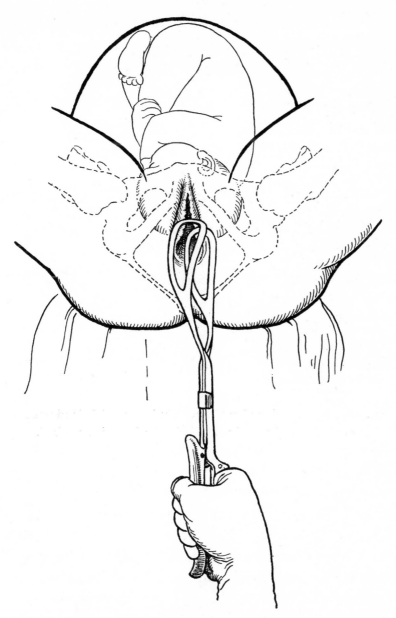

FIG. 45. Orientation. Position of Kielland forceps on L.O.T.

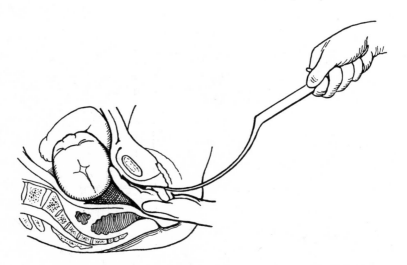

Fig. 46.   Introduction of anterior, right blade of Kielland forceps
to anterior, right ear in L.O.T. by the inversion method.

lowered in the midline to the level of the horizontal. When the heel of the blade has passed under the symphysis, the handle has been further depressed to an angle of about forty-five degrees below the horizontal and the fenestration has reached its destination opposite the anterior cheek. The higher the head is in the pelvis, the lower the handle will be below the horizontal, and the further into the uterus the blade will have to be inserted (Fig. 47).

Since the blade has been introduced in the inverted manner, its cephalic curve is directed away from the head toward the anterior wall of the uterus. It must now be rotated so that its cephalic curve will coincide with the curve of the head. Rotation of the blade is on its own axis *away* from the occiput toward the midline and toward the knob. This is accomplished by the right hand grasping the handle and the thumb pressing against the side of the finger guard opposite the button, turning it counterclockwise with a twist of the wrist over an arc of 180 degrees, until the button points toward 3 o'clock. As the rotation is being completed, the handle is depressed slightly in order to follow the plane of least resistance (Fig. 48). If the blade is rotated in the wrong direction, that is, *toward* the occiput, the high point of the toe rubs against the anterior wall of the uterus and may cause damage.

Rotation is never persisted in if resistance is encountered. The blade may not be inside the cervix, or if inside the cervix, it may not be far enough, or may be too far inside the uterus. Resistance to both introduction and rotation may also be encountered if a low contraction ring is present. Introduction of the blade carries more risk than rotation because

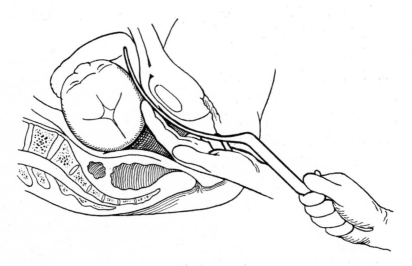

Fig. 47.   Anterior right blade of Kielland forceps in place
opposite the anterior right ear in L.O.T. with its cephalic
curve directed away from the head.

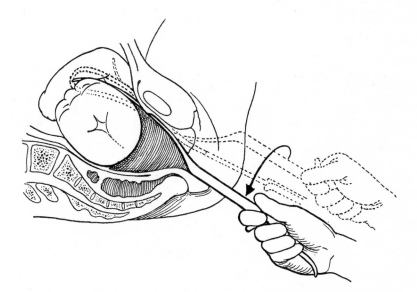

Fig. 48. Rotation of anterior, right blade of Kielland forceps counterclockwise in L.O.T. so its cephalic curve will coincide with the curve of the head.

in rotation the beveled edge will not cut the uterus, but lift it away from the head. Whereas in introduction, the toe may be forced through a thin lower uterine segment.

Wandering Method of Application

If it is found impossible to rotate the anterior blade after it is inside the uterus, the inversion method of application of the Kielland forceps is abandoned and the anterior blade is applied by the gliding or wandering maneuver, carrying it around the face to the anterior ear, as in the classical instrument (Fig. 49A). If the head is well flexed, interference often is encountered in wandering the blade around the side of the face. This may be avoided by "reversing" the maneuver and *wandering* the same blade, *upside down,* around the side of the occiput (Fig. 49B). In the belief that the wandering method is less hazardous than Kielland's inversion method, some operators prefer to use it exclusively. However, if the inversion method is not used, the same disadvantages accompanying the use of the wandering method with the classical instrument are encountered.

Direct Method of Application

Occasionally the head is so low in the pelvis in the transverse position that it is difficult and even impossible to apply the anterior blade of the Kielland forceps by either the inversion or the wandering method. This situation is encountered when the head is near the outlet, in the transverse position with an anterior parietal presentation. Because of the asynclitism and depth of engagement, the anterior ear can be

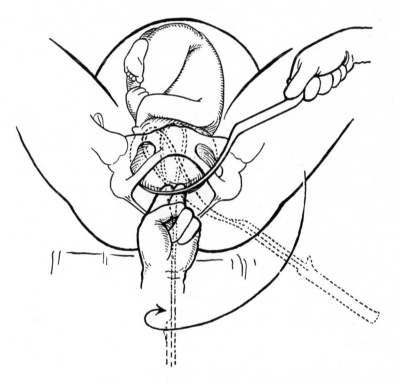

FIG. 49A. The "wandering maneuver" for application of the anterior, right blade of the Kielland forceps to the anterior, right ear of L.O.T.

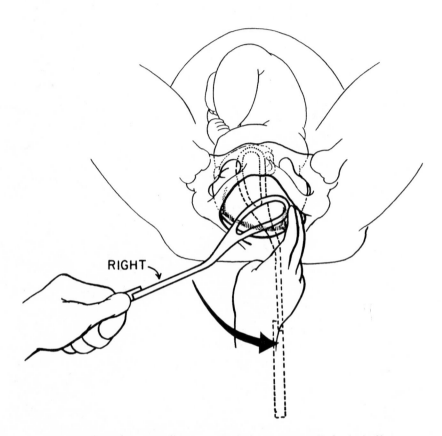

FIG. 49B. The "reverse wandering maneuver" for application of the anterior, right blade of the Kielland forceps held, upside down, in the left hand, inserted to the left side of pelvis and wandered, counterclockwise, to anterior, right ear of L.O.T. with flexed head.

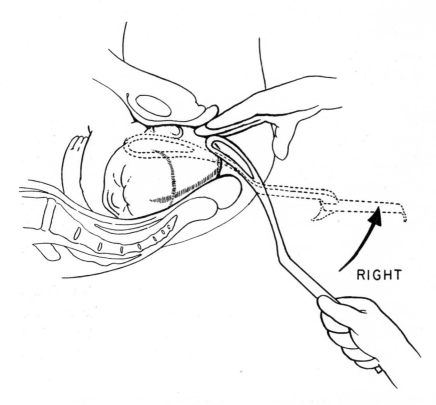

RIGHT

FIG. 49C. "Direct application" of anterior, right blade of
Kielland forceps to anterior, right ear of L.O.T. Vertex near
perineum with marked anterior parietal presentation.

palpated vaginally, just behind the symphysis. Here a direct application is required.

In the direct application, the anterior blade—the right blade for an L.O.T. and the left blade for an R.O.T.—is applied first directly under the symphysis to the anterior ear (Fig. 49C). The approach is from below upward, with the handle pointing toward the floor below the edge of the table. The concaved, bevelled surface of the blade is in contact with the anterior parietal bone and the toe is directed under the symphysis toward the anterior ear. With gentle upward insertion, the blade slides up to the desired location on the anterior cheek. After the posterior blade is applied in the usual manner for a transverse position, the asynclitism is corrected by elevation and equalization of the locked handles. This is followed by instrumental anterior rotation, check of application, and traction.

The posterior or left blade is introduced next. It is always introduced posteriorly between the shank of the anterior blade and the patient's right thigh, regardless of the method of application of the anterior blade. This obviates the necessity of crossing the handles in order to lock them. Four fingers, palm up, are introduced inside the vagina posterior to the head in order to reach the posterior lip of the cervix. If the cervix is fully retracted only two fingers are inserted as a guide, thereby avoiding the risk of displacement of the head. The blade with the cephalic curve up is passed directly behind the head along the palmar surface of the guiding hand (Fig. 50). More difficulty may be encountered with the introduction of this blade than the anterior, owing to the obstruc-

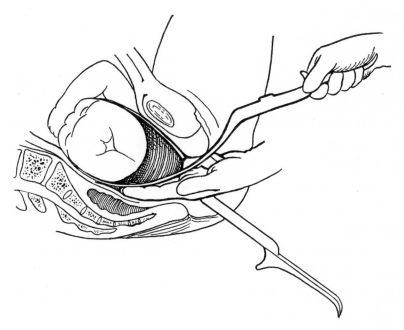

FIG. 50. Introduction of posterior, left blade of Kielland forceps
directly to the posterior, left ear in L.O.T.

tion that may be caused either by the cervix or the promontory. If resistance is met, the handle of the posterior blade may be moved up and down, with a jiggling motion as it is inserted, in order to bring the toe inside the cervix and keep it hugging the head. When the blade is opposite the posterior or left ear the shanks are locked (Fig. 51). The sliding lock permits this at any level on the shank. One handle may be at a higher level than the other owing to an asynclitic application. Traction is made on the finger guard which is nearer the perineum. Simultaneously, pressure is applied in the opposite direction to the other finger guard until the handles are equalized, thus correcting the asynclitism. If the posterior blade cannot be inserted far enough to permit locking, the use of extra force should be avoided. Downward traction on the handle of the anterior blade against the head should cause the latter to descend on the inclined plane of the cephalic curve of the posterior blade far enough to allow the handles to be locked. After a preliminary check of the application the head is rotated counterclockwise ninety degrees to the anterior-posterior (O.A.) diameter of the pelvis. Because of the reverse pelvic curve of the Kielland forceps, rotation is not over a wide arc but almost directly on the axis of the shanks with depression of the handles at the completion of the turn (Fig. 52).

If resistance to rotation of the head is encountered in a normal pelvis it may be due to failure to depress the handles into the axis of the pelvis; extension of the head; or the head may be too high in the pelvis. Flexion is accomplished, first, by readjustment of the forceps so that the plane of the shanks

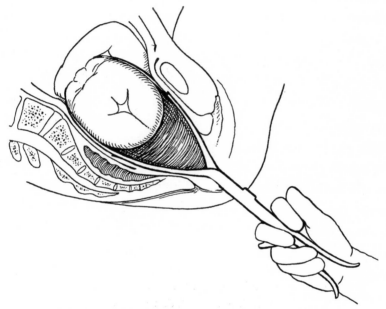

FIG. 51. Kielland forceps applied to L.O.T.

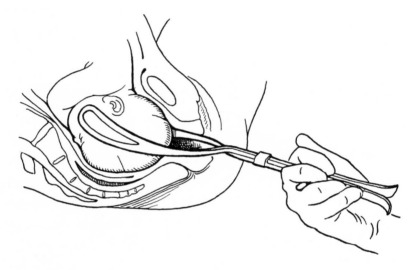

FIG. 52.   Kielland application after counterclockwise
rotation of L.O.T. to O.A.

is within a finger's breadth mediad of the posterior fontanelle. Then the handles are compressed and carried laterally to the midline. If the head is near the inlet it will have to be drawn down in the transverse position to the plane of the greatest pelvic dimension before rotation can be accomplished. However, traction is not applied if the bulge of the anterior blade is not below the symphysis. *Traction with the head in the transverse diameter of the inlet is contraindicated if the bulge of the anterior blade is above the symphysis, because it exerts force against the symphysis and the bladder.*

If such a situation is met, the procedure depends largely upon the type of pelvis present and the size of the child. If the pelvis is of the flat type, the Kiellands are contraindicated. The delivery may be accomplished with the Barton forceps, by version, or if disproportion not previously established seems probable, by cesarean section provided the condition of the child is good. The pelvis may have a straight sacrum or forward jutting upper sacral segment shortening the antero-posterior diameter. Here again, the Barton forceps offer the best results following the necessary traction in the transverse position, past the point of obstruction, before anterior rotation can be done. In other types of pelves, especially the anthropoid, the head must be rotated above the inlet. The subsequent traction is on an unengaged head.* The risk of

---

* Instrumental elevation of the occiput posterior, prior to anterior rotation *above* the inlet, followed by traction is rarely justified. The one indication for such a procedure is an anthropoid pelvis without disproportion—one in which there is insufficient room to permit anterior rotation, because of the short transverse diameter throughout. When faced with this situation the next move is to attempt delivery as an occiput posterior without anterior rotation. For this a Simpson type of axis-traction forceps is preferable. If this fails the only alternative with forceps is elevation of the head above the inlet with the Kielland forceps, followed by anterior rotation and traction. (*Footnote continued on p. 124.*)

such a procedure in most cases makes version or cesarean section preferable. However, version, a very valuable operation under proper conditions, has become increasingly less popular in recent years.

This is most unfortunate as the art of version is being neglected. Without practice, skill is undeveloped and without skill gained with experience and tempered by good judgment, version should not be attempted after a failure with forceps. It is much wiser and safer to choose cesarean section.

Today, cesarean after an attempted forceps delivery does not carry the same risk as it did a few years ago. On very rare occasions this procedure is justified and indicated, when, during an attempt at delivery through the vagina, it seems apparent that further efforts from below will result in serious or irreparable damage to the baby and severe injuries to the mother.

If immediate delivery seems necessary and a proper attempt, with not too much and not too little effort, with forceps, in experienced hands, is unsuccessful further efforts in this direction should cease. Of course it is much better to make the correct decision in advance, but in some border-line cases this is not always possible.

If an attempt with forceps seems indicated, the important factor lies in what constitutes a proper attempt. One may make too little effort at application, rotation or traction and

---

(Footnote continued from p. 123.)

Success has been achieved on occasions in selected cases but it is not recommended as a routine.

This maneuver is contraindicated in other types of pelves because of the shorter anteroposterior diameter of the inlet. Cesarean section is usually preferable.

stop too soon with an inadequate attempt. On the other hand one may be reluctant to stop before exhausting all his strength. Not infrequently in certain cases, when expert help was obtained, the delivery was successfully accomplished without undue effort. In other instances the operator, who at first was unsuccessful, soon after, had complete success with another type of instrument. Then there are those patients who delivered spontaneously after having been put back to bed following failure of attempted forceps delivery.

The proper decision of when to abandon further effort with forceps depends on the judgment, skill, and experience of the operator.

Traction

After rotation has been completed, the application is rechecked and if found to be correct, traction is begun. Traction, which is a backward pull in the direction of the handles, is aided by the modified Saxtorph or Pajot maneuver. The finger guards are encircled by the middle and index fingers of the right hand, with the palm up (Fig. 53). After the head has reached the outlet, an episiotomy is done in most cases and the legs are lowered to give further relief of tension on the perineum. As the posterior fontanelle is delivered, the handles are elevated gradually during traction to the horizontal. The technic is similar to that of the classical instrument, except that it is important never to elevate the handles of the Kielland forceps above the horizontal, because the backward pelvic curve of the blade may cause a sulcus tear. In order to gain more extension a special maneuver may be employed. Pressure is applied to the fundus by the assistant to keep the head from receding. The handles are unlocked and depressed, one at a time, toward the floor so that the plane of the shanks is two or three fingers' breadth below the posterior fontanelle. The handles are then locked and elevated to the horizontal while slight traction is being made. This maneuver causes extension of the head without digging the toes of the blades into the sulci. It may be repeated as often as necessary in order to gain the required extension necessary for the performance of the Ritgen maneuver. The blades are then removed, taking the top or right blade off first, following the technic of the classical type of instrument. Sometimes difficulty will be experienced in removing the blades. This may be due to a loop of cord which has been caught in the fenestration, or pressure from a narrow outlet. Rather than use undue force, it is advisable to deliver the head with one or both blades still in place.

R.O.T. Position

In the R.O.T. position the left ear is anterior, so the left blade, which is the anterior blade and has the lock on it, is applied first (Fig. 54). It is applied under the symphysis, inside the cervix, and into the uterus, as already described (Figs. 55 and 56). It is rotated in a clockwise direction away from the occiput toward the midline, until the button on the handle points toward the patient's right leg at 9 o'clock (Fig. 57). The posterior blade is applied between the shank of the anterior blade and the right thigh, as in the L.O.T. position (Figs. 58 and 59). The head is rotated clockwise to the anterior position. The application is rechecked and, if found

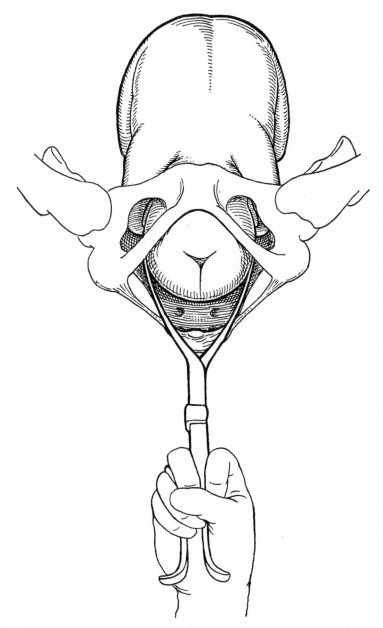

FIG. 53. Traction on O.A. after anterior rotation with
the Kielland forceps.

satisfactory, traction is applied and delivery is completed (Fig. 60).

It is contraindicated to apply traction with the Kielland forceps to a head arrested transversely at the inlet, with a posterior parietal presentation, because the bulge of the anterior blade is above and behind the symphysis. This presentation suggests the presence of a flat pelvis or a disproportion which simulates the mechanism of a flat pelvis. Traction in this instance applies the force directly against the symphysis and the anterior wall. The result is likely to be a separation of the symphysis and injury to the bladder. Before traction is applied to a head in the transverse position, the anterior parietal bone should be far enough below the superior straight so that the bulge of the anterior blade can be seen below the symphysis.

Kielland Forceps Applied to Posterior Positions

L.O.P. Position

Assuming that the posterior fontanelle is at 4 o'clock, the blades are held locked in the position in front of the patient which they will occupy when applied. Therefore, the knobs point toward 4 o'clock. The anterior (right) blade is grasped and the posterior (left) blade is temporarily discarded. The anterior blade is introduced under the symphysis to the anterior or right ear in the same manner as when applied to a direct transverse position. After insertion it is rotated away from the occiput and toward the midline in a counterclockwise direction, until the knob on the finger guard points toward 4 o'clock. The rotation in this instance is over an arc

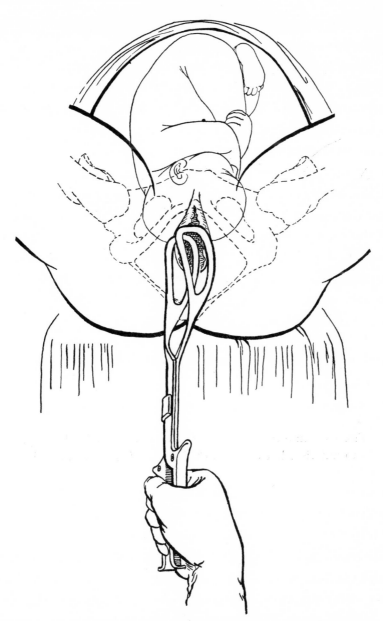

FIG. 54. Orientation for position of Kielland forceps on R.O.T.

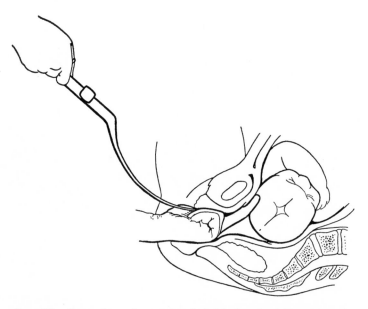

FIG. 55.   Insertion of anterior, left blade of Kielland forceps
to anterior, left ear of R.O.T. by the inversion method.

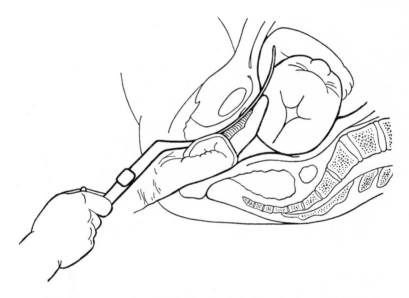

FIG. 56.   Anterior, left blade of Kielland forceps opposite
anterior, left ear of R.O.T.

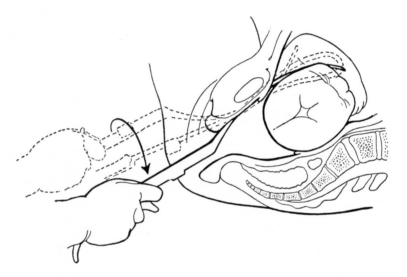

FIG. 57.   Clockwise rotation in R.O.T. of anterior, left blade
of Kielland forceps so that its cephalic curve will coincide
with the curve of the head.

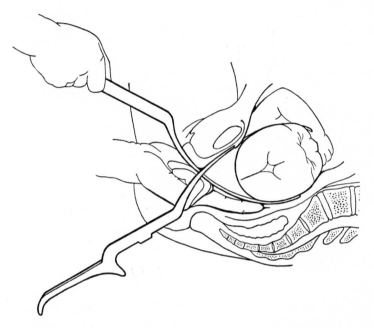

FIG. 58. Application of posterior, right blade of Kielland forceps directly to posterior, right ear of R.O.T.

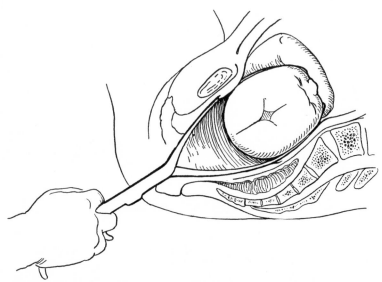

FIG. 59. Kielland forceps applied to R.O.T.

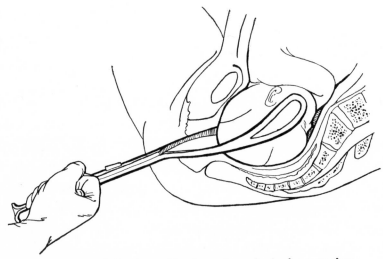

FIG. 60. Kielland application after clockwise rotation
of R.O.T. to O.A.

of about 135 degrees to the posterior oblique position of the head, instead of the 180 degree arc in the transverse position.

Resistance to rotation of the inverted anterior blade, which is known to be inside the cervix, may often be overcome by carrying the handle away from the midline toward the occiput. The posterior blade is then inserted in the same manner as in the transverse position, except that the blade is introduced posteriorly in the oblique diameter, parallel to the sagittal suture, so that it will pass directly to the posterior ear. Then, after locking the handles, asynclitism is corrected by pulling down on the finger guard which is nearer the patient's perineum, and by pushing up on the other. The head is then flexed and rotated counterclockwise over an arc of about 135 degrees to the anterior position. The application is checked and traction is applied as previously described.

R.O.P. Position

The occiput is assumed to be at 8 o'clock. The right ear is posterior and the left ear is anterior, so the left or anterior blade, the one with the lock on it, is introduced first. The introduction is the same as in the R.O.T. position but after clockwise rotation, away from the occiput, the knob on the handle instead of pointing to 9 o'clock, as in the transverse position, points to 8 o'clock. The posterior or right blade is inserted posteriorly as in the L.O.P. position, except that it follows the opposite oblique diameter parallel to the sagittal suture. The handles are locked, asynclitism is corrected, the head is flexed and rotated clockwise to the anterior position and extraction is performed in the usual manner.

Kielland Forceps Applied to Direct Posterior Position
Upside-Down Direct Application

In cases with the occiput in the hollow of the sacrum and the posterior fontanelle between 5 and 7 o'clock, the inversion method of applying the anterior blade is abandoned. Instead the reverse or upside-down direct application is made with the knobs facing the floor. The main exception to this procedure is an anthropoid pelvis, in which the transverse diameter is too narrow to permit anterior rotation. In this case the occiput is delivered as a posterior without rotation. The approach for the reverse application is from below, upward, with the handles at an angle of about 45 degrees below the horizontal, and the application is made directly to the sides of the head. In order to facilitate locking, the right blade, the one without the lock, is always introduced first, to the left side of the pelvis, opposite the right ear regardless of the position.

L.O.P.—O.P. Position

The occiput is at or between 5 and 6 o'clock. With the head in this position it is important to know on which side the back lies, so that when the head is rotated it will be turned to the side on which the back lies, thereby preventing injury to the child's neck. If the operator has followed the case in labor he should know to which side the head should be rotated in order to prevent injury. Palpation of the small parts may aid in the decision, or a tentative trial at rotation may show the direction of least resistance.

The blades are inserted from the kneeling or sitting posi-

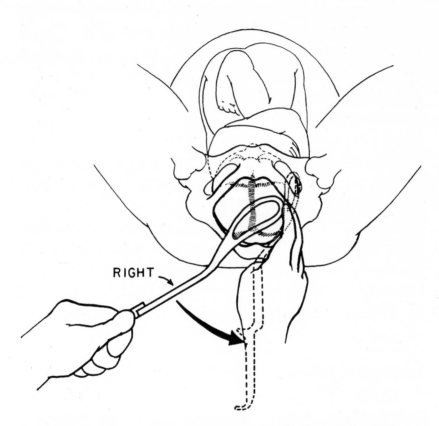

RIGHT

FIG. 61. The "upside-down direct" application of the Kielland forceps for O.P. The right blade with the anterior surface of its shank pointing downward is held in the left hand and introduced to the left side of the patient's pelvis directly to the infant's right ear.

tion with the toes of the blades pointing backward. A direct application is made from below upward. Holding the blades with the toes inverted and the knobs pointing to 5 or 6 o'clock, the right blade is taken in the left hand and is inserted to the left side of the vagina directly to the right ear (Fig. 61). The left blade is taken in the right hand, inserted to the right side of the vagina over the child's left ear. After locking, the head is flexed by elevating the handles. The blades are then rotated anteriorly counterclockwise, the occiput passing through 3 o'clock. At the same time, pressure is made on the left side of the uterus by the assistant, in an attempt to rotate the shoulders of the child as the head is being rotated. When rotation has been completed to a point at 12 o'clock, application of the forceps is checked and if found satisfactory, traction is made in the axis of the pelvis. The head is extracted by the usual Kielland technic.

R.O.P.–O.P.

Assuming the occiput to be at or between 7 and 6 o'clock, the operator assumes a kneeling or sitting position in front of the patient and holds the forceps locked and inverted in a position which he wishes them to assume when applied, with the knobs at or between 7 and 6 o'clock. The right blade is taken in the left hand with the toe of the blade pointing backward. It is inserted from below, upward to the left side of the vagina, over the child's right ear. The left blade is taken in the right hand with the toe of the blade pointing backward and is inserted into the right side of the vagina over the child's left ear. The head is flexed by elevating the locked handles. Clockwise rotation is then performed so that the occiput passes through 9 o'clock and finally comes to a position at 12 o'clock. While rotation of the head is being accomplished, the assistant exerts pressure on the right side of the uterus in an attempt to rotate the child's shoulders. The application is checked, traction in the axis of the pelvis is made, and the head is delivered in the usual Kielland manner, care being taken not to elevate the handles above the horizontal, since these forceps have a reverse pelvic curve.

This upside down direct application technic for the O.P. position is not to be used unless the head is well down in the pelvis, almost, if not on the perineum. When the head is higher, the reverse pelvic curve on the Kielland forceps interferes with a good application. The procedure of choice is to rotate the head manually to an L.O.P. or R.O.P. as indicated, carrying the occiput as far toward the transverse position as possible. Then the Kielland inversion method of application for the new position is used.

CHAPTER 9

Special Instruments *(Continued)*

KIELLAND FORCEPS APPLIED TO FACE PRESENTATION*

Anterior Chin

IN FACE presentation with the chin anterior, a direct application to the sides of the face is allowed with the Kielland or a classical type such as the Tarnier, because of its excellent axis traction. Since the chin replaces the occiput as the presenting part, another exception to one of the cardinal points of forceps application arises. The left blade, instead of being applied to the left ear, is applied to the right ear. The left blade, held in the left hand, is inserted into the left side of the vagina over the child's right ear and the right blade, held in the right hand, is inserted into the right side of the vagina over the child's left ear. The application is checked, using the mouth as the landmark in place of the posterior fontanelle. Traction is made downward, preserving complete extension until the chin is born under the symphysis. The

---

* See Gomez, H. E., and Dennen, E. H.: Face presentation. A study of 45 consecutive cases. Obst. & Gynec. 8:103 (July) 1956.

handles are then elevated gradually to the horizontal with traction so that the occiput is delivered over the perineum and the head is born by flexion.

Transverse Chin — R.M.T.

In all face presentations the chin takes the place of the occiput and the Kielland forceps is applied accordingly. In an R.M.T. position the application is the same as for an R.O.T. The left or anterior blade is inserted first, under the symphysis to the right or anterior ear, by the inversion method. Rotation of the left blade is clockwise toward the midline away from the chin. The right blade is then inserted directly posterior to the left or posterior ear between the handle of the left blade and the patient's right thigh. The shanks are locked and clockwise rotation of the chin towards 12 o'clock is performed bringing it under the symphysis. Downward traction is made after checking the application and the head is delivered by flexion, the chin being born first under the symphysis.

Transverse Chin — L.M.T.

In an L.M.T. position the application is the same as for an L.O.T. Therefore, the right blade is inserted under the symphysis between the cervix and the child's left or anterior ear (the second exception to the cardinal rule of left blade to left ear), the toe of the blade being carried into the uterus in the inverted manner (Fig. 62). The blade is then rotated counterclockwise away from the chin, toward the midline

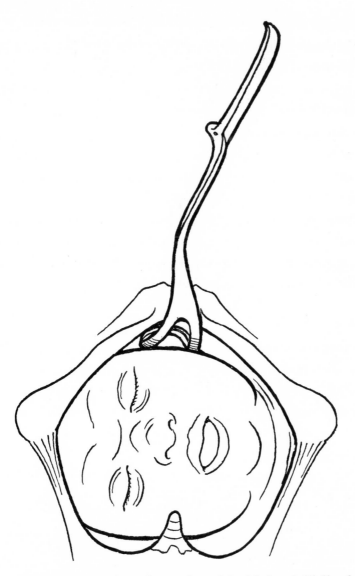

Fig. 62. Insertion of anterior, right blade of Kielland forceps to anterior, left ear of a face presentation, L.M.T., by the inversion method.

and toward the knob (Fig. 63). The left blade is inserted directly posterior and the shanks are locked. Rotation of the head in a counterclockwise direction brings the chin under the symphysis. Depression of the handles at the completion of rotation assures complete extension. Traction and delivery are accomplished as in an anterior chin position (Fig. 64).

If the inversion method of application is thought inadvisable, the anterior blade may be applied by the wandering maneuver.

When the station of a transverse chin presentation is in the upper pelvis near the plane of the inlet, rotation cannot be accomplished until the head has been brought down to the midplane by traction in the transverse diameter.

Posterior Chin

A posterior chin cannot be delivered as such with any degree of safety. Rotation to anterior is necessary before traction is applied. The Kielland technic for a posterior chin position is similar to that of an occiput posterior position in the hollow of the sacrum. Holding the blades upside-down, with the knobs facing the floor, the operator assumes the kneeling or sitting position. The right blade, the one without the lock, held in the left hand is inserted from below upward to the left side of the pelvis over the left ear. The left blade, the one with the lock, held in the right hand is inserted from below to the right side of the pelvis and over the right ear. The shanks are locked and elevated slightly to preserve extension. The chin is rotated to the symphysis clockwise in an R.M.P. position and counterclockwise in an

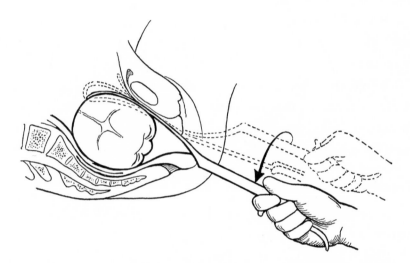

FIG. 63. Counterclockwise rotation of an anterior, right blade of the Kielland forceps to anterior, left ear of a face presentation, L.M.T., so that its cephalic curve will coincide with the curve of the head.

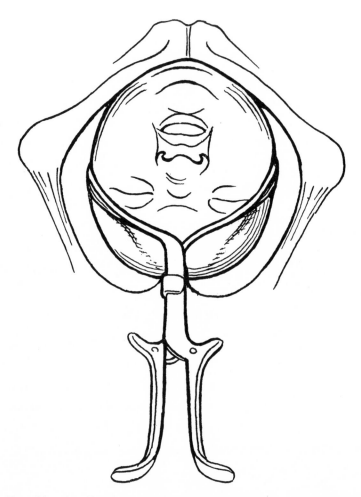

Fig. 64. Application of Kielland forceps to an anterior chin, ready for traction, after counterclockwise rotation of a face presentation, L.M.T. to M.A.

L.M.P. Traction and delivery are the same as in an anterior chin presentation.

If the chin is in the posterior oblique position of an L.M.P. or an R.M.P., but not well down in the hollow of the sacrum, the technic of application of the Kielland forceps is the same as for an L.O.P. or R.O.P., respectively. The chin takes the place of the occiput, and the mouth replaces the posterior fontanelle. After anterior rotation of the chin, traction is applied. Preliminary to this, it is of vital importance to rule out disproportion.

The same contraindications for the Kielland forceps in occiput presentations apply for the face. These are a flat pelvis or a deformed sacrum shortening the anteroposterior diameter of the pelvis. Here again, the Barton forceps are required.

BROW PRESENTATION*

The Kielland forceps is used occasionally for brow presentation. When used, the head is either flexed or extended so as to change the brow to an occiput or face presentation. The pivot point of the fetal head in brow presentations is not in the center of the forceps blades. Therefore, traction tends to increase the extension. Poor results attending forceps deliveries of brow presentations are common. Version or cesarean section is usually preferable.

KIELLAND IN PLACE OF A CRANIOCLAST

If craniotomy is indicated, the Kielland forceps may be applied to fix the head while the fontanelle is punctured

---

* See Moore, E. J. T., and Dennen, E. H.: Management of persistent brow presentations. Obst. & Gynec. 6:186 (Aug.) 1955.

with the Smellie scissors. Compression of the head is accomplished by squeezing together the handles of the Kielland forceps with a towel tied around them, or by using a set-screw crossbar attachment to the ends of the handles designed for this purpose by Riediger. Rotation and extraction may be accomplished without changing the application. If it is thought that the blades will slip from the cephalic application, the frontal occipital application may be used. Since the sliding lock permits locking at any level on the shanks, a short blade on the occiput and a long blade on the face can be obtained.

METHODS OF APPLICATION OF KIELLAND FORCEPS

The methods of application of Kielland forceps are listed in the order of frequency of indicated use:

1. *Inversion:* For transverse and posterior positions except the direct O.P.

    This is indicated in most anthropoid and android pelves and all except the simpler cases in a woman with a gynecoid pelvis. The contraindications are: a platepeloid pelvis, especially one with a posterior parietal presentation; a straight or deformed sacrum shortening the A-P diameter of mid pelvis; unavoidable resistance or obstruction to the use of this maneuver; a direct occiput posterior position: and a transverse position with an anterior parietal presentation well down in the pelvis.

2. *Wandering:* For transverse positions.

    This is indicated when the inversion method meets resistance. Since the head is usually incompletely flexed, the anterior blade is wandered around the side of the face. The contraindications are the same as those given for the inversion method.

2A. *Reverse Wandering:*
When the head is well flexed the anterior blade is wandered around the side of the occiput, thereby avoiding resistance caused by the forehead.

3. *Direct:* For transverse positions near the outlet with an anterior parietal presentation.
The anterior blade is inserted directly (not inverted) to the anterior cheek and ear, which can often be palpated behind the symphysis. The direct method is rarely used on anterior positions because a classical type of forceps is preferable.

3A. *Upsidedown Direct:* For direct occiput posterior positions near the outlet.
The blades are applied upside down, directly to the sides of the head. This method is used with caution on android and anthropoid pelves. Some have insufficient room for anterior rotation of the occiput. These require delivery "as an occiput posterior."

The standard method of application in most instances is the "inversion method." This provides the main advantage of the Kielland, namely: a single, accurate application without displacement, and it can be accomplished without undue hazard because the instrument has a backward pelvic curve.

The term "classical method," instead of the more specific

term "inversion method," has crept into the literature and into case histories. This term should be avoided, since it has led to confusion, being misinterpreted as referring to the classical method used for applying a classical type of forceps. When referring to the Kielland, it suggests the "wandering method" and not the standard procedure by "inversion."

CHAPTER 10

Special Instruments *(Continued)*

BARTON FORCEPS

DR. LYMAN G. BARTON of Plattsburg, N. Y., designed his forceps for application to heads arrested in the transverse diameter of the inlet, especially those with a posterior parietal presentation. The instrument may be used to advantage in deep transverse arrest, posterior position, and face presentation. The forceps was presented in 1925. Much of the credit for its popularity is due to Caldwell and Studdiford, and to Bachman.

Construction

One blade is attached to the shank by a hinge, making it flexible over an arc of ninety degrees. The other blade has a deep cephalic curve. The blades are attached to the shanks laterally at an angle of about fifty degrees, so that when the forceps is held in the anterior position there is no pelvic curve. However, when it is rotated over an arc of ninety degrees to the transverse position, the angle of attachment of the blades to the shanks forms a perfect pelvic curve. The

151

lock is of the sliding type. There is a separate traction handle that can be applied to give axis traction.

Advantages

The thin hinged blade affords an easy and accurate application by the wandering maneuver to transverse heads, particularly those having a posterior parietal presentation. The hinge allows the blade to be wandered around the head into place in front of the anterior ear behind the symphysis. With a fixed blade, it is impossible to obtain this application to a posterior parietal presentation because the anterior parietal bone overrides the symphysis.

The sliding lock allows for correction of asynclitism, as locking can be accomplished at any level on the shank.

The lateral attachment of the blades to the shanks forms a perfect pelvic curve when applied to a transverse head. Thus, descent to low-mid pelvis may be accomplished safely by traction in this diameter before rotation.

The traction handle gives good axis traction.

The most important indication for the use of this instrument is a flat pelvis with a head arrested at the inlet in the transverse diameter with the posterior parietal bone presenting. Here the only instrument that can be used with safety is one which has a flexible blade attachment which allows the blades to conform to the curve of the pelvis when applied to a transverse head. This permits traction in the transverse diameter. This applies also to pelves with a straight or forward jutting upper sacrum, shortening the anteroposterior diameter of the mid pelvis.

Disadvantages

A disadvantage attached to this instrument is the possibility of its slipping when used on a difficult case, owing to its lightness and flexibility. Another disadvantage is that frequently it is necessary to remove the forceps after rotation and apply a classical type of instrument for the extraction. The reason for this is that after rotation to anterior, the Barton has no pelvic curve, without which extension over the perineum requires much more effort for delivery. Also after rotation, the handles are directed obliquely away from the long axis of the patient. This makes traction awkward even with the axis-traction handle.

The Barton forceps is undesirable in android and anthropoid pelves. Here, because of a transverse contraction, descent of the head must occur in or near the anteroposterior diameter. The Barton is constructed to give traction for descent in the transverse position. Immediate rotation followed by traction with this instrument, in these pelves, requires much more effort. As a result injuries to the vagina are frequent.

TECHNIC

Transverse Positions L.O.T. and R.O.T.

The hinged blade is the anterior blade and is always introduced first. It is applied by the wandering maneuver either over the face or occiput until it reaches the anterior-malar-parietal region under the symphysis (Figs. 65 and 66). When applied, the hinge should be close to the sagittal suture, one finger's breadth mediad to the posterior fonta-

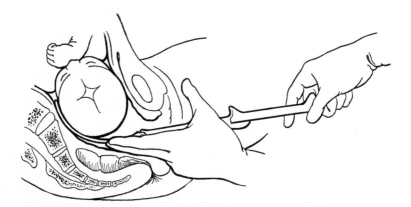

FIG. 65.   Introduction of the first or hinged blade of the
Barton forceps for L.O.T. with *partial extension* (both fon-
tanelles can be felt with equal ease).   The handle is held
in the *right* hand and the index and middle fingers of the
left hand are at the heel, after guiding the toe of the blade
directly posterior to the head.

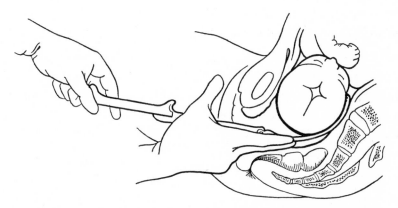

FIG. 66. Introduction of the first or hinged blade of the Barton forceps for R.O.T. with *partial extension.* The handle is held in the *left* hand and the index and middle fingers of the right hand are at the heel, after guiding the toe of the blade directly posterior to the head.

nelle. If the head is extended, less resistance is encountered
if the blade is wandered over the face (Fig. 67); if flexed, the
blade is wandered over the occiput (Fig. 68). The higher
the head, the more important it is to insert the anterior
hinged blade directly posterior in order to make sure the
blade is inside the cervix before wandering it around to the
anterior. The posterior blade is then inserted directly
posterior between the handle of the anterior blade and the
patient's right thigh. The deep scoop of the posterior blade
keeps the toe of the blade hugging the head, thereby avoiding the posterior lip of the cervix and the promontory of the
sacrum (Figs. 69 and 70). The anterior blade usually is
further up in the pelvis than the posterior. However, no
difficulty in locking is encountered since the sliding lock permits this maneuver to be carried out at any level on the shank.
In locking, the handle of the posterior blade, which is at or
above the level of the horizontal, should not be depressed but
the handle of the anterior hinged blade should be elevated to
meet it. Traction on the under finger guard, combined with
the modified Pajot maneuver, simultaneously corrects asynclitism and lowers the station of the head (Figs. 71, 72, 73 and
74). The traction handle is attached to the shanks between
the finger guard and the lock, with the screw-head adjacent to
the grooved surface of the under finger guard. Further traction, with the head in the transverse position, may be necessary in order to bring the head well down into the plane of
the greatest pelvic dimension before rotation is attempted
(Figs. 75 and 76). Rotation is counterclockwise for an L.O.T.
presentation and clockwise for an R.O.T. to the anterior

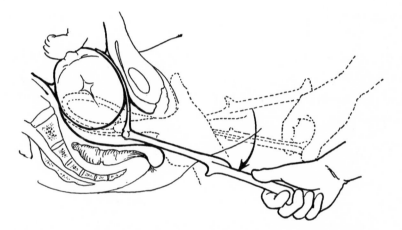

FIG. 67. The hinged Barton blade has been "wandered" by
the index and middle fingers of the *left* hand, around the
right side of the pelvis over the *face* of an *extended* L.O.T.,
to the anterior, right ear behind the symphysis. The *right*
hand on the hinged handle changes its level as the blade
approaches the anterior ear.

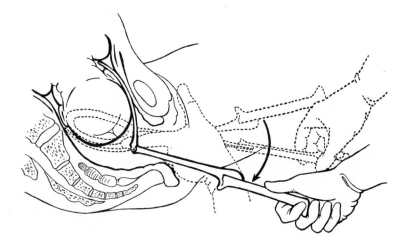

FIG. 68. The hinged Barton blade has been "wandered" by the index and middle fingers of the *left* hand around the *right* side of the pelvis over the *occiput* of a *flexed* R.O.T. to the anterior, left ear behind the symphysis. The handle is held in the *right* hand. If this R.O.T. had been *extended,* the hinged instrument would have been held in the *left* hand and "wandered" by the fingers of the *right* hand, around the *left* side of the pelvis over the *face* to the anterior, left ear.

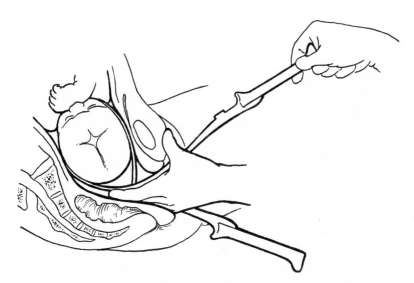

FIG. 69. Introduction of posterior, rigid blade of Barton forceps, between the handle of the anterior, hinged blade and the right thigh, directly to the posterior left ear of L.O.T.

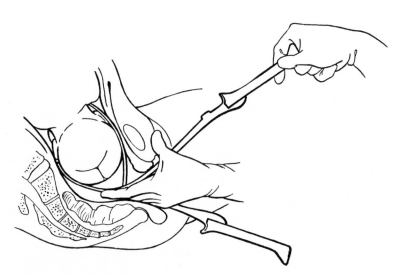

Fig. 70. Introduction of posterior, rigid blade of Barton forceps between the handle of the anterior, hinged blade and the right thigh, directly to the posterior right ear of R.O.T.

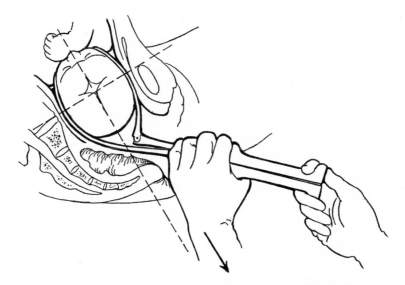

FIG. 71. Application of Barton forceps to L.O.T. Any asynclitism had been corrected by equalizing the handles.

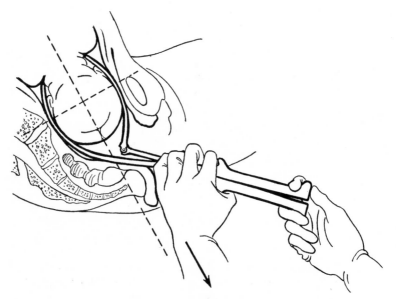

FIG. 72.   Application of Barton forceps to R.O.T.

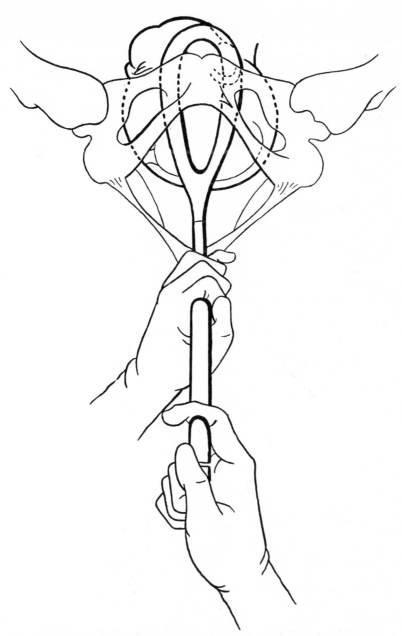

FIG. 73. Front view of Barton forceps applied to L.O.T.

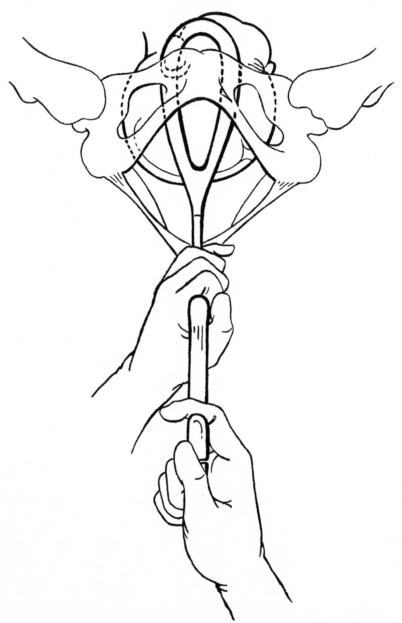

Fig. 74. Front view of Barton forceps applied to R.O.T.

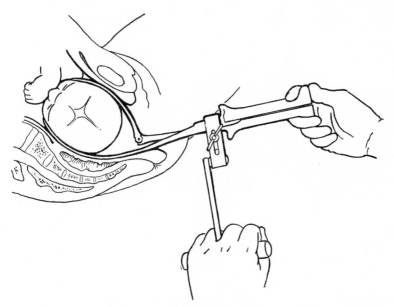

FIG. 75. Barton forceps with axis-traction handle, ready for traction on L.O.T. Anterior rotation is not done, until the head is near the outlet.

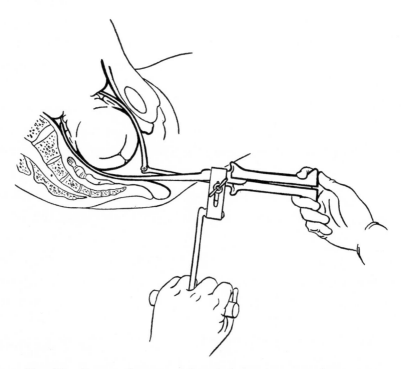

F𝗜𝗀. 76. Barton forceps with axis-traction handle ready for
traction on R.O.T. without anterior rotation, until head is
well down in the pelvis.

position. The handles are rotated over a wide arc using the center of the head as a pivot point (Figs. 77 and 78). At the completion of rotation, the handles are parallel to or a little below the horizontal, directed obliquely away from the midline toward the opposite side, that is, after rotation of an L.O.T. to anterior, the handles are near the patient's right thigh; and after rotation of an R.O.T., the handles are near the left thigh (Figs. 79 and 80).

Traction is applied by one hand in the direction of the shank of the axis-traction handle. The other hand grasps the handles of the forceps to guide the direction of the force and to aid in extension during the traction. In a primipara, resistance to extension over the perineum is encountered frequently even after an episiotomy and lowering of the legs. This is due to the loss of the availability of the pelvic curve of the instrument after anterior rotation. In such a case, the Barton forceps is removed after descent and rotation have been accomplished, and a classical instrument is applied to complete the delivery.

The chief indication for the Barton forceps is the chief contraindication for the Kielland forceps, that is, high transverse arrest with posterior parietal presentation, especially in a flat pelvis. The necessary traction in the transverse diameter cannot be made with the Kielland instrument on this type of case, as in this position, its pelvic curve and axis traction cannot be utilized. The bulge of the anterior blade would cause injury to the symphysis and the bladder. In the presence of a straight sacrum, shortening the anteroposterior diameter of midpelvis, the risks are more pronounced. On the

Fig. 77.   Barton forceps on L.O.T. with head near the outlet
preparatory to counterclockwise rotation to O.A.

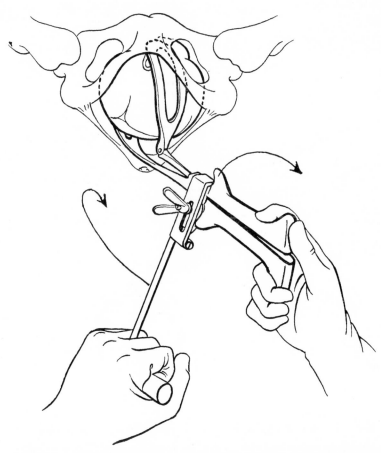

Fig. 78. Barton forceps on R.O.T. with head near the outlet preparatory to clockwise rotation to O.A.

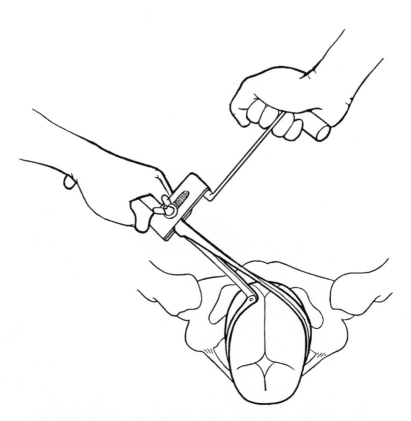

FIG. 79. Barton forceps on O.A. after descent and counter-clockwise rotation from L.O.T. to anterior, ready for traction and extension. The handles are directed away from the midline toward the right thigh.

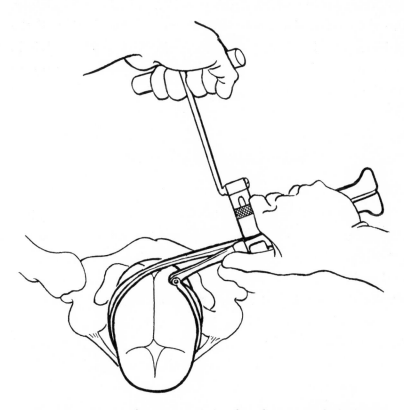

FIG. 80. Barton forceps on O.A. after descent and clockwise rotation from R.O.T. to anterior, ready for traction and extension. The handles are directed away from the midline toward the left thigh.

other hand, it is possible to make traction with the Barton forceps to this position because, when applied, it has an excellent pelvic curve and good axis traction. The force, therefore, is in the axis of the pelvis away from the symphysis and the bladder. The head can be drawn well down in the pelvis in the transverse diameter, even into the outlet, if necessary, to pass the point of obstruction before anterior rotation can be done.

POSTERIOR POSITIONS

L.O.P.

In the L.O.P. position the hinged anterior blade is applied first, directly to the anterior ear, instead of by the wandering maneuver as in the transverse position. It is held in the left hand and is guided by two fingers of the right hand to the left anterior side of the pelvis just in front of the right or anterior ear. An assistant holds it in place. The handle of the posterior blade is held in the right hand and the toe is guided to the right posterior side of the pelvis to the right side of the promontory, just in front of the left or posterior ear.

After locking and equalizing the handles and attaching the traction bar, counterclockwise rotation is performed over a wide arc of 135 degrees until the posterior fontanelle is directly under the symphysis at 12 o'clock and the handles are opposite the right thigh at 9 o'clock. Traction is now applied in the usual manner. If it is found that much effort is necessary for extraction, the Barton forceps should be removed and a suitable classical type substituted.

R.O.P.

The technic of application to an R.O.P. is similar to that of the L.O.P. except that the order of the sides is reversed. The hinged blade, held in the right hand, is inserted first, directly to the right anterior side of the pelvis opposite the left or anterior ear. The posterior blade, held in the left hand, is inserted directly to the left posterior side of the pelvis opposite the right or posterior ear. The rotation is clockwise to anterior, with the handles finally pointing obliquely away from the midline at the level of 3 o'clock.

The best results with this instrument on posterior positions are obtained when the head is well down in the pelvis. If the head has to be brought down in the posterior position with the forceps to a lower level before it can be rotated, the Barton forceps loses most of two of its advantages present in transverse arrest, a good pelvic curve and good axis traction. Hence, incomplete rotation as far as the transverse position should be done as soon as possible. Traction is continued in this position until the head has reached the level of the ischial spines or lower before completing the rotation to the anterior position.

The exceptions to this maneuver are android and anthropoid pelves. With a short transverse diameter of the pelvis, traction should be made on a head in the anteroposterior diameter. Under these conditions the Kielland forceps is much more effective.

CHAPTER 11

Piper Forceps for the After-coming Head

THIS FORCEPS was designed by Edmund B. Piper of Philadelphia in 1924 for use on the aftercoming head of breech deliveries.

Construction

The long shanks have a backward curve at about the middle. This drops the handles to a considerable distance below the level of the blades. The other chief difference in the shanks is the development of individual planes. The plane of the shanks is in the same plane as that of the blades to a point about 5 cm. (2 inches) from the lock, whereas the lower 5 cm. (2 inches) are in the plane of the handles. In the classical instrument, the plane of the shank is in the same plane as that of the handle throughout its entire length. This unique type of construction of the shanks in the Piper forceps gives more spring to the blades. Consequently, with more spring to the blades, there is less compression of the head. The blade is a modification of the Tarnier instrument, having a small cephalic and slight pelvic curve.

Advantages

The dropped handles allow a direct application to the sides of the head without elevating the body above the horizontal, thereby preventing injury to the child's neck.

The spring of the blades, made possible by the long portion of the shanks lying in the same plane as the blades, causes less compression of the head.

The backward bend of the shanks gives axis traction.

Disadvantages

The blade has a straight pelvic curve and may cause some damage to the outlet during extension if an episiotomy is not done. This is a minor consideration since the straight pelvic curve is necessary in order to make a direct application to a high head. The spring in the blade along with the slender almost straight cephalic curve causes slipping on a large round head or if the application is not accurate.

TECHNIC

After the shoulders and the arms have been delivered and the head is in the pelvis with the chin posterior, if any delay is encountered in delivering the head, the Piper forceps should be applied. The left blade is applied first, in order to avoid difficulty in locking. The assistant carries the body and arms of the child toward the mother's right side, holding them at or slightly above the horizontal. The body must never be extended over the symphysis unless the baby is "face to pubis." * With the child's body carried toward the right side, the approach to the left side of the pelvis is more direct and less difficult.

The operator assumes a kneeling or sitting position in front of the patient. The left blade, held in the left hand, is inserted to the left side of the pelvis over the child's right ear (the third exception to the cardinal point of left blade to the left ear for forceps application) (Fig. 81). If the head is in the anteroposterior diameter, the left blade goes directly to the side of the pelvis. If the head is in the L.O.A. or right oblique diameter, the left blade is the posterior blade. When the head is in the R. O. A. or left oblique diameter, the left blade is the anterior blade. In each instance the left blade is applied first, directly to the side of the head. The handle of the forceps is held almost at right angles to the patient, near her right thigh, beneath the body of the child, while the toe of the blade is guided into the vagina with two fingers of the right hand. The handle is swept in an arc toward the midline, while the toe of the blade passes into the pelvis along the side of the child's head to its right ear. The assistant then carries the body of the child toward the patient's left thigh, exposing the approach to the right side of the pelvis. The right blade is similarly introduced by the right hand to the

---

* In the "face to pubis" situation, if a bi-manual maneuver fails to deliver the aftercoming head, the forceps is applied. The approach is from below upward, under the baby's back, directly to the sides of its head, the leading point of which is now the occiput. Following traction, the occiput is delivered over the mother's perineum with the chin facing the pubis. Simultaneously the legs and body are carried up over the symphysis.

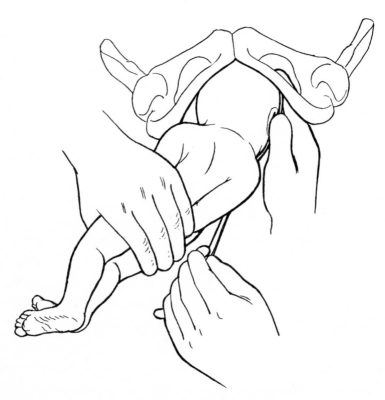

Fig. 81.   Insertion from below upward of first or left blade of the
Piper forceps to the right ear of the aftercoming head.

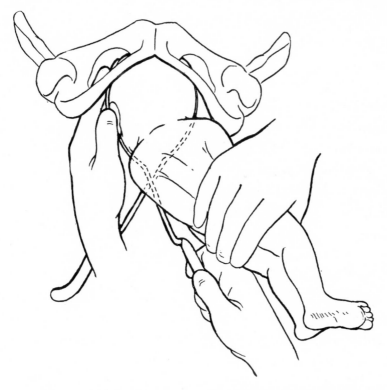

Fɪɢ. 82. Insertion of second or right blade of Piper forceps
to the left ear of aftercoming head.

right side of the pelvis opposite the child's left ear (Fig. 82).
If resistance is met, the toe of the blade is introduced more
posteriorly and wandered around to the side of the head.
After the shanks have been locked, the child is allowed to
straddle the forceps. The handles rest in the up-turned palm
of the right hand with the middle finger in the space between
the shanks.

After application of the forceps, if the head is not in a
direct anterior position, it is rotated instrumentally and
downward traction is made from the kneeling or sitting position in the direction of the handles until the chin appears at
the outlet. The handles are then elevated with traction in
order to conform to the curve of the pelvis and to promote
and preserve flexion during delivery of the head over the
perineum. While making traction, the right thumb grasps
the child's thigh over the forceps handles, so that when the
head is extracted, it will not fall through the blades. The
index and middle fingers of the left hand press on the suboccipital region, splinting the neck and helping to bring the
occiput under the arch (Fig. 83). If resistance is encountered
at the outlet after an episiotomy has been done and the legs
lowered, the handles of the blades are depressed and elevated
during gentle traction in a pump-handle maneuver. This
favors delivery of the head over the perineum with less effort
and less injury; first, by bringing the suboccipital region
further under the arch, and second, by increasing the flexion.
Finally, extraction is done with the handles in the horizontal,
delivering the head with forceps still in place (Fig. 84).

Usually application of the forceps is not made until the

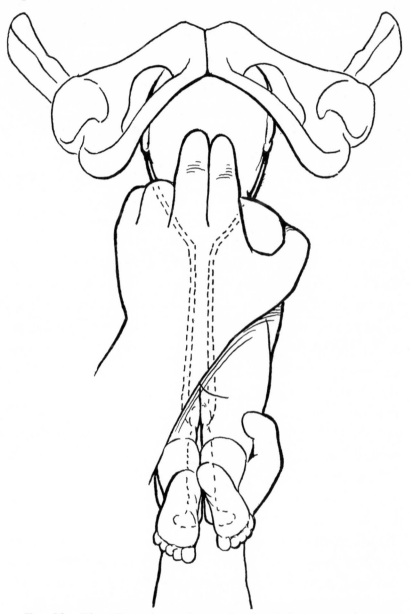

Fig. 83. Piper forceps on aftercoming head during traction. Body resting on shanks, leg clamped to handle by thumb, handles resting in upturned palm of right hand with middle finger in the space between the shanks at the lock, neck splinted by fingers of the left hand.

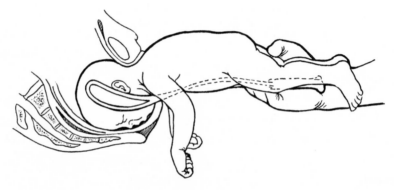

FIG. 84. Application of Piper forceps to aftercoming head which is about to be delivered over perineum by flexion without removal of the forceps.

head is well in the pelvis. The question arises why the Piper forceps is needed after the head is low in the pelvis. The reason is that in a partially extended head it is difficult to get the head out without injury, unless instrumental flexion is used. Also in a contracted outlet, or with a pelvis which has sharp ischial spines, a low symphysis, or a prominent coccyx, difficulty in extracting the head without the use of forceps may cause injury to the neck by traction from below and injury to the tentorium by manual pressure from above. With the use of the Piper forceps, less effort is necessary and the force is applied to the most resistant part of the child's body, namely, the bimalar, biparietal region.

A classical type of forceps may be used on the aftercoming head but its disadvantages make it undesirable. The pelvic curve and the straight shanks require elevation of the child's body toward the symphysis to permit application of the blades beneath it. This risks injury to the neck and tends to extend the head. Also the body against the forward bend of the shanks and handles interferes, in some cases, with complete instrumental flexion of the head. The rigid blades give more compression to the head. Unless the instrument has such an attachment, axis traction is lacking.

If the disadvantages of the Piper forceps in any individual case are apparent, there are alternatives which can be used to advantage.

The Hawks-Dennen forceps, with similar principles of construction to the Piper, has less spring in the blades than does the Piper and an ample cephalic curve suitable for large heads. The reverse or backward pelvic curve and the sliding lock of the Kielland forceps favor a direct and accurate application and a good line of traction. Both the Hawks-Dennen and the Kielland forceps have been used successfully following failure with the Piper forceps.

CHAPTER 12

Choice of Instrument

GIVEN A proper case for delivery with forceps, an operator may select the kind of instrument most suitable for the conditions. Delivery may be accomplished with only one, or at most two varieties of forceps. However, other things being equal, a greater degree of success should be obtained with a knowledge of the advantages, and a discrimination in the use of the various kinds of forceps. There are several kinds of forceps, old and new, that have peculiar advantages under certain conditions.

In delivery with forceps under proper conditions, there are two features of prime importance: the application of the forceps to the child's head, and the traction used in accomplishing the delivery. These two acts determine the manipulation, effort, and consequently, the associated trauma.

APPLICATION OF FORCEPS

The application must be cephalic and accurate. In a true cephalic or biparietal application, the blades should fit the

185

head, as accurately as possible. They should lie evenly against the sides of the head, reaching from the parietal bosses to, and beyond, the malar eminences, covering symmetrically the spaces between the orbits and the ears. There should be no extra pressure at any one point.

A correct application is essential. It prevents injury to the head because: the blades fit the head accurately and pressure is evenly distributed; the pressure is on the least vulnerable areas; the increased diameter of the head, due to the thickness of the blades, is at the narrowest place, thereby minimizing the force necessary for delivery.

A correct application lessens injury to the mother because the head advances in the proper attitude. It is vital to the technic of the delivery because it enables the operator to know the exact position of the head, and allows him to use the most favorable diameters. These conditions are not fulfilled by the undesirable brow-mastoid application.

In selecting an instrument with which a good application can be obtained, the choice depends upon a correct diagnosis of the amount of molding, position, station, and attitude of the head, and the type of pelvis.

On molded heads, the best application is obtained with blades which have a long, tapering, cephalic curve. Those with a short, full curve do not fit evenly, causing pressure points, and often are not anchored below the malar eminences, with consequent cutting or slipping.

In considering the position of the head, the instrument to be chosen is the one which gives the correct application with the least effort. When the occiput is anterior, the application is, as a rule, easily made, and any blade which fulfills the requirements of the molding may be used. For other positions and presentations there are special types which will be considered with the various forceps operations. A head in the upper part of a flat pelvis or in a pelvis with a straight sacrum may be angulated in such a position that a cephalic application cannot be obtained unless the forceps has a flexible blade.

TRACTION

Traction also plays a very important part in the choice of the forceps. To use the least force, one should make traction in the pelvic axis. This may be done manually but is best accomplished in all stations of the head with some form of axis-traction forceps. Even in low forceps, axis traction is valuable in obtaining flexion, and in eliminating the force wasted against the symphysis. The deep episiotomy allows the handles of the forceps to lie in a lower plane. This, with the use of the fingers as a fulcrum, may eliminate the necessity of instrumental axis traction on low heads. However, the axis-traction instrument automatically directs the force away from the symphysis, and thus simulates the physiological mechanism of labor.

Axis traction suggests, to many, a difficult operation with a complicated instrument. For this reason, in the average case it is often neglected, though the advantages are admitted. The classical forceps, without axis traction, are frequently used with the maximum force, reduced by the modified Pajot maneuver. Axis-traction forceps, however, tend to keep the force in the plane of least resistance, thereby diminishing the amount of effort and injury.

SELECTION OF INSTRUMENT

In the selection of an instrument which fulfills the requirements of application and traction, there are many excellent forceps from which to choose. Some are simple, others complicated. All have one or more good points which justify their use when properly chosen. Some are so similar that there is very little choice between them. Most modern forceps of the classical type follow, in a general way, one of two constructions: the shanks overlap and the blades have a short, cephalic curve as in the Elliot; or the shanks are separated and the blades have a long, tapering curve as in the Simpson. But not all of them have axis traction. This disadvantage can be overcome in some of the Elliot type by the use of the Bill axis-traction handle.

Various localities have their favorites. In Boston and its vicinity, the light Good forceps with the traction rods from the fenestrations concealed in the handles is popular. So is Irving's forceps, with traction rods similar to Tarnier's, permitting the use of the most accurate line of traction of any axis-traction attachment. In Philadelphia, there is a preference for the DeWees, and Piper's modification of it, with the traction rod attached to the end of one handle. Chicago favors the DeLee modification of the Simpson without axis traction, and the Adair, with multiple perforations of the solid blades. In New York, several types find favor: DeWees', DeLee's, Tucker-McLane's, Bailey-Williamson's, Lobenstein-

Tarnier's, Elliot's, and Hawks-Dennen's. In different parts of the United States, the Kielland's and Barton's are gradually increasing in popularity for use in cases with the head not in an anterior position. The interest in both these instruments should continue to grow with the better understanding of their advantages and a thorough knowledge of the technics of their use (Figs. 85, 86, 87, and 88).

LOW FORCEPS

In a truly low forceps, most heads are in the anterior position. The amount of molding, and the type of outlet determine the choice of instrument. In pelves with a low pubic arch, and a short anteroposterior diameter of the outlet, it is essential to choose a blade with a good pelvic curve. This will put less pressure on the perineum, and will tend to avoid sulcus tears of the vagina during extension. In normal pelves, the important factor is protection of the child's head against cuts and abrasions. Third degree tears are guarded against by frequent use of perineotomy. It is thought that a cut perineum, well repaired, is better than one which is torn or stretched. Perineotomy also relieves the pressure on the anterior wall.

The mother is, as a rule, a primipara, or perhaps a multipara in long labor. This usually means molding of the baby's head, with its sides lengthened and flattened. A Simpson type of forceps fits best. It has a long, shallow, cephalic curve, and the tips can be anchored well below the malar eminences, preventing pressure points and slipping. A blade with a short,

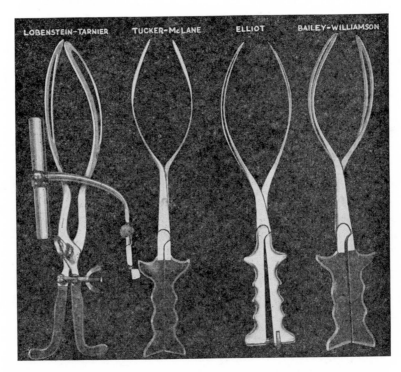

FIG. 85.   Examples of Elliot type forceps, with
overlapping shanks (except Tarnier).

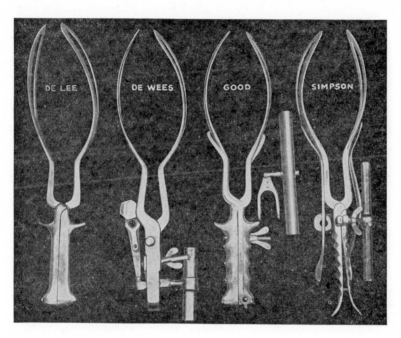

FIG. 86. Simpson types of forceps with separated shanks.

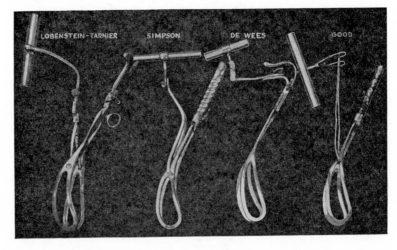

FIG. 87.   Axis-traction attachments on Simpson
types of forceps.

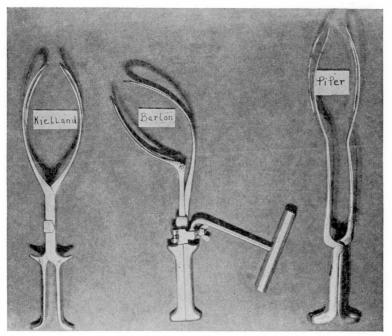

Fig. 88. Special types of forceps.

sharp, cephalic curve, of the Elliot type, is suitable for round
heads. When considerable molding is present, it fits unevenly,
and occasionally gives difficulty in proper locking.

For easy extractions, the solid blades of the Tucker-
McLane are popular with some obstetricians. They are easy
to apply and remove, and may be used on small round heads.
On molded heads, they may slip, due to lack of anchorage
below the malars, and they exert pressure on two points, the

Fig. 89.   Hawks-Dennen forceps with perineal curve
for axis traction.

zygoma, and parietal boss. The result may be a cut over the
zygoma just in front of the ear, and the appearance later of
swelling over the boss. The latter is a periostitis which may
last for weeks, and occasionally develops into an abscess.
Luikart's modification, in which the outline of the fenestration is preserved on the inner surface of the solid blade, minimizes this disadvantage.

Many times, what is thought to be an easy low forceps later
proves to be the caput of a molded head, the biparietal diameter of which is at, or above, the ischial spines. Then the
operator wishes he had chosen a fenestrated blade originally.

The solid blades are excellent as rotators in the first stage of the Scanzoni maneuver. A suitable fenestrated type may be used for the extraction.

To simplify the choice of instrument for anterior positions of the occiput at any station in the pelvis, an uncomplicated, light, fixed axis-traction forceps has been designed by Everett M. Hawks and Edward H. Dennen (Fig. 89).

Several principles are included in this instrument. The advantages of application and traction tend to make the delivery easier and safer. The modified Simpson blades, with the Kielland cushion, tend to fit the head without pressure points or cutting; and they do not slip, because the tips can be anchored well below the malar eminences. The exaggerated pelvic curve of the posterior lips of the blades permits extension over the perineum with the least amount of pressure on the posterior vaginal wall and sulci. The modified Piper shanks give more spring to the blades, allowing accommodation to heads of different sizes and shapes, with the least amount of compression. The backward curve of the shanks gives axis traction.

LOW-MID AND MID FORCEPS

In the low-mid and mid forceps operations, more frequently than in the low, the position, as well as the shape of the head, must be considered in selecting a suitable type of instrument. The rules for anterior positions are the same in all stations of the head, with emphasis on axis traction. The DeWees forceps gives excellent fixed axis traction and is considered the choice by many. With the head in transverse arrest, some operators have developed their skill in the use of manual rotation, and also the gliding or wandering maneuver. However, it is not an uncommon experience to find a head which cannot be rotated manually without displacement; or one which refuses to remain anterior during the process of applying the second blade, and locking the handles. In the gliding maneuver, the anterior blade occasionally hits the brow, causing the occiput to rotate backward. This may result in a brow-mastoid application which no amount of manipulation will entirely correct. To simplify this procedure, two special types of forceps have been developed, the Kielland and the Barton. Their chief advantage is the ease with which an accurate cephalic application can be obtained. Both have the sliding lock principle which allows for adjustment on asynclitic heads. The Kielland, since it is built for traction, has a wider field of usefulness, and appears to be the choice, except in pelves with a straight sacrum. However, the Barton, though less effective as a tractor, often requiring another type to complete the delivery, is chosen by some because its technic of application is simpler.

In posterior positions the single accurate application, without displacement of the head, and semi-axis-traction pull with the Kielland favor better results, with less manipulation than the Scanzoni, Pomeroy, and "Key in Lock" maneuvers or manual rotation. Also the dangers of version in unfavorable cases are avoided. The Barton forceps may be used, but the advantage of rotation and traction with the Kielland in most cases makes it the choice. The solid blades are desirable in some cases. The Jacobs model should be popular since it eliminates the need of reapplication after rotation.

This applies also to the directly posterior occiput when well down in the pelvis. The upside down, direct application of the Kielland to the sides of the head permits rotation and extraction without readjustment of the blades. The exceptions are a marked anthropoid and a marked android pelvis in which, because of limited space, it is considered necessary to deliver the posterior occiput, as such, without anterior rotation. Here a Simpson type with axis traction is preferable in order to satisfy the requirements for molding, and for the need of an instrument with a good pelvic curve.

The backward or reverse pelvic curve of the Kielland forceps is a disadvantage in extraction through a narrow outlet with a low symphysis. Unless one is familiar with the special technic for extension with this instrument, it is thought best to remove the forceps after anterior rotation has been completed, and the head flexed and fixed with one or two tractions, substituting a suitable axis-traction forceps of the classical type with a good pelvic curve. This keeps the force in the axis of the pelvis, and lessens the danger of injury to the posterior wall and perineum and to the pubic ramii. Following the proper use of the Kielland forceps, rarely, if ever, are there any badly marked faces or facial palsies. The beveled surface or cushion on the inside of the blades eliminates the cuts and bruises, and the brow-mastoid application is avoided by using the inversion method of application. Much has been said about the dangers of the Kielland, but, as is true of any instrument, the dangers diminish as the knowledge of its proper use increases. Complicated cases have frequently been made simple by the Kielland, even after unsuccessful attempts with other types.

HIGH FORCEPS

As a rule, a high forceps should be avoided. But occasionally in well chosen cases, with version contraindicated, it offers less risk than cesarean section. When the head is arrested in or just below the superior straight, the same principles which apply to mid forceps are used, with one exception. This is a flat pelvis, with the head in the transverse position, and the posterior parietal bone presenting. Here, as was so well shown by Caldwell, the Barton forceps stands alone as the choice. The ease of application diminishes the amount of manipulation; the perfect pelvic curve reduces the amount of effort and minimizes the amount of injury; and the sliding lock permits adjustment as the asynclitism is corrected. If, in addition to a flat inlet, there is also a straight sacrum, shortening the A-P diameter of the mid pelvis, the contraindication to any forceps except the Barton is more pronounced. This principle applies regardless of the station of the head in transverse arrest.

The Kielland forceps is not chosen because when applied to this type of case its pelvic curve and axis traction cannot be utilized. It increases the angulation of the head, and consequently, the diameter of the descending part is increased. The necessary preliminary traction in the transverse diameter to bring the head into low-mid pelvis before it can be rotated

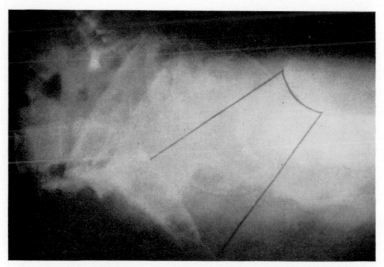

FIG. 90.   Straight sacrum with forward jutting sacral seg-
ment shortening the A-P diameter of mid pelvis.   (From
Dennen, E. H.: Choice of forceps. Clin. Obst. & Gynec.
Vol. 2, Courtesy of publisher, Paul B. Hoeber, Inc.)

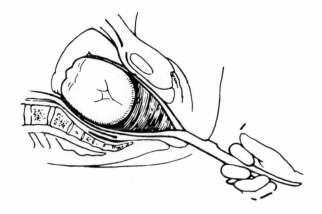

FIG. 91. Kielland forceps applied to L.O.T. in straight sacrum. Anterior rotation is not possible. Traction is inadvisable, if not contraindicated. (From Dennen, E. H.: Choice of forceps. Clin. Obst. & Gynec. Vol. 2. Courtesy of publisher, Paul B. Hoeber, Inc.)

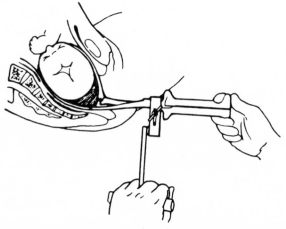

F<small>IG</small>. 92. Barton forceps ready for traction on L.O.T. in
straight sacrum. Anterior rotation is not done until head
reaches outlet following traction. (From Dennen, E. H.:
Choice of forceps. Clin. Obst. & Gynec. Vol. 2. Courtesy of
publisher, Paul P. Hoeber, Inc.)

endangers the symphysis pubis and bladder, against which most of the force is directed. Hence, the chief indication for the Barton forceps is also the main contraindication for the Kielland (Figs. 90, 91 and 92).

The Mann forceps* and the Miseo forceps, both with flexible blades and a split universal joint, may be used to advantage. After more general use, these unique instruments may prove to be the closest approach to the long sought for universal forceps.

In face presentations, the advantages of the Kielland forceps again make it the choice. This is particularly true when the chin is directly posterior. Here the blades may be applied upside down directly to the sides of the head, with the pelvic curve directed backward. Then rotation of the chin to anterior, followed by extraction, may be done without readjustment of the forceps.

For the aftercoming head in breech extractions, the Piper forceps are the choice. The springy blades permit adjustment to heads of different sizes and shapes, with the least amount of compression. The dropped handles make it easy to obtain an application directly to the sides of the head with-

---

* No longer available.

In 1956, Dr. John Mann presented a new instrument. In its construction he abandoned the split universal joint with flexible blades of his first instrument, for a more classical type of forceps with rigid blades and parallel shanks. The new forceps has a special wedge-shaped lock which is split in two; each half may slide up and down on the corresponding shank, thus permitting adjustment of asynclitism and allowing separation of the shanks and blades for accommodation to heads of different sizes. This instrument appears to have advantages over the classical forceps, but not over the Kielland or the Barton when use of either of these is truly indicated.

out raising the body above the horizontal. The backward bend of the shanks gives axis traction.

SUMMARY

1. In a proper case for delivery with forceps, the two essential requirements are: an accurate cephalic application, and traction in the axis of the pelvis.

2. A correct diagnosis must be made of the amount of molding, position, station, and attitude of the head, and type of pelvis.

3. Molded heads require a blade with a long, shallow cephalic curve, as in the Simpson type. On round heads the Elliot type fits best.

4. Axis traction diminishes the amount of effort and injury, and is desirable in any station of the head.

5. The large variety of instruments in use shows that there is no universal forceps.

6. In the majority of anterior positions, the Simpson type of blade, with some form of axis traction, is desirable.

7. A traction curve forceps designed by Hawks and Dennen, combining features of several instruments and satisfying the requirements of application and traction, may be used on anterior heads.

8. In most transverse and posterior positions, the Kielland forceps seems to be the choice. Rotation manually, or with the Barton or the solid blades, may be used in some cases.

9. A high transverse head, with a posterior parietal presentation in a flat pelvis, requires the Barton forceps. This

applies also to the deformed sacrum shortening the A-P diameter of mid pelvis.

10. In most face presentations, especially with the chin posterior, the Kielland forceps offers advantages.

11. On aftercoming heads, the Piper forceps is the choice. The Hawks-Dennen or the Kielland may be substituted with advantage, especially on a large head well down in the pelvis.

MORTALITY: RESULTS

Following the policies of forceps deliveries, outlined on the preceding pages, results at the New York Polyclinic Hospital from 1946 through 1960 were as follows:

Of 18,121 total viable births, forceps were employed in the delivery of 10,405 patients. The application of forceps was recorded as: 15 high, 670 mid, 5442 low mid, and 4278 low.

There were three maternal mortalities, all following a low forceps, Simpson type, delivery. Two of the deaths were due to hemorrhage and one to bilateral pheochromocytoma with metastasis to the thyroid gland.

The total number of fetal and infant deaths was 103, a mortality of just under 1 per cent (0.990 per cent). By excluding macerated babies and those having major congenital anomalies the mortality figure was corrected to 0.58 per cent (61 deaths).

With high forceps there was one, a macerated stillborn child, delivered from a diabetic mother; hence, the mortality associated with high forceps delivery is correctable to zero.

The total fetal and infant loss associated with mid forceps delivery numbered 16 or 2.38 per cent, correctable in the same manner as employed above to 11 or 1.64 per cent.

With the application of low-mid forceps, the total fetal and infant mortality was 0.99 per cent (54 deaths), corrected to 0.62 per cent (34 deaths), and for low forceps it was 0.74 per cent (32 deaths), corrected to 0.37 per cent (16 deaths).

Table 1 shows a comparison between the fetal and infant mortality results of all viable deliveries and those following all spontaneous viable births, during the same time, with those deliveries by forceps.

Table 1

STATION	NO. OF FORCEPS DELIVERIES	FETAL AND INFANT MORTALITY No.	Per Cent	CORRECTED FETAL AND INFANT MORTALITY No.	Per Cent
High	15	1	6.66	0	0.00
Mid	670	16	2.38	11	1.64
Low Mid	5442	54	0.99	34	0.62
Low	4278	32	0.74	16	0.37
Total	10405	103	0.99	61	0.58

	NO. OF SPONTANEOUS DELIVERIES	FETAL AND INFANT MORTALITY No.	Per Cent	CORRECTED FETAL AND INFANT MORTALITY No.	Per Cent
Viable births	5348	136	2.54	50	0.93

	NO. OF DELIVERIES (ALL METHODS)	FETAL AND INFANT MORTALITY No.	Per Cent	CORRECTED FETAL AND INFANT MORTALITY No.	Per Cent
Total viable births	18121	365	2.01	191	1.05

Although the aforementioned policies have been followed closely by the attending, courtesy, and house staffs, exceptions are inevitable. They are due perhaps to a failure to appreciate all of the factors involved in the individual patient, differences in opinion regarding certain policies, deliberate intent to test policies, or to extenuating circumstances. Certain of the exceptions served to prove the point, however, and the policies as outlined have seemed to stand the tests of time and use.

There were failures with the Tucker-McLane forceps followed by success with the DeWees, failures with the Simpson and Elliot types and success with the Kielland forceps, and failures with the Kielland instrument and the delivery completed successfully with the Barton forceps. It rarely, if ever, took more than one such experience to convince the operator that there is indeed a choice of forceps to suit the case.

CHAPTER 13

Conclusion

THE CHOICE of instrument is the one which gives the best application with the least manipulation and the best line of traction with the least effort. The choice is dependent upon the shape, position, station, and attitude of the head, and the type of pelvis.

On molded heads in the anterior position, the long tapering cephalic curve of the Simpson type forceps is the choice, on round heads the Elliot type fits best. The axis-traction principle is desirable at any station of the head in the pelvis and the higher the head, the more imperative it is that the forceps have some form of axis-traction attachment. This will tend to direct the pull in the axis of the pelvis and lessen the force necessary for delivery.

When the occiput is in the transverse position, it is necessary to rotate it to anterior, either manually or instrumentally. Following manual rotation the Simpson type of forceps is chosen, since molding is usually present. Instrumental rotation of the occiput transverse may be accomplished with a classical or a special type of forceps. If the classical instrument is used the choice is the Elliot type. The overlapping shanks and the short, round, cephalic curve take up less space and meet fewer points of obstruction during the wandering maneuver for applying the anterior blade than do the separated shanks and long tapering cephalic curve of the Simpson type. After anterior rotation, one may proceed with traction, accepting the disadvantage of an Elliot type on a molded head for the more important advantage of a better application with less manipulation.

Unfortunately, there is a high percentage of bad results with both the manual and the classical forceps rotations. The commonest of these is a brow-mastoid application, so often accompanied by facial markings and less frequently by intracranial injury. Repeated attempts to correct a brow-mastoid application may cause displacement of the head forcing the operator to abandon the forceps for some other procedure previously considered more hazardous or not indicated. The incidence of poor results can be reduced markedly by the use of a special type of forceps, the Kielland or the Barton. The advantages of the Kielland make it the choice in most cases, depending on the type of pelvis. These advantages are: (1) a single accurate application without displacement by the inversion method, (2) the beveled inner surface minimizing facial injuries, (3) the sliding lock permitting adjustment of asynclitism since the handles can be locked at any level on the shanks, and (4) a semi-axis-traction pull due to the reverse pelvic curve. The Kielland is particularly indicated in android and anthropoid pelves, with the Barton contraindicated. Its wide field of usefulness makes it desirable in all but the simpler cases with a gynecoid pelvis. The main exceptions to the Kielland forceps are a flat pelvis or one with a deformed sacrum shortening the anteroposterior diameter of mid pelvis. Here, the Barton forceps stands alone as the choice.

In such a case, the mechanism requires descent in the transverse with asynclitism, past the point of deformity, before anterior rotation can be accomplished. The only instrument in common use, constructed to correct asynclitism and give good traction on a head in the transverse position is the Barton. Hence, the main indication for the Barton, flat pelvis or straight sacrum, is the chief contraindication for the Kielland. Many of the bad results following the use of the Kielland occurred in these pelves.

In the forceps management of the occiput posterior there are four accepted methods:

1. *Manual rotation* to anterior, including the digital and Pomeroy maneuvers. Following manual rotation the choice of instrument because of molding is the Simpson type, preferably one with some form of axis traction, such as the DeWees, Irving, Good, Milne-Murray, Haig-Ferguson, Hawks-Dennen, and others.

2. *Combined manual and instrumental rotation* to anterior. After the rotation has been carried out manually as far as the transverse position it is completed instrumentally. The forceps is applied by the wandering maneuver using

the Elliot or one of its types, such as the Bailey-Williamson or the solid blades of Tucker-McLane or Luikart.

3. *Instrumental rotation* of an occiput posterior to anterior may be done with the classical forceps or with one of its hinged modifications, such as the Jacobs or LaBreck, also the Miseo with the split universal joint. The Elliot type is preferable.

In doing the modified Scanzoni maneuver, the choice is the Tucker-McLane forceps with the Bill axis-traction handle. If one anticipates a short application with consequent slipping of a short, round blade not anchored well beyond the malar eminence of a long molded head, he may substitute a Simpson type for the traction.

In some districts the DeLee "Key-in-Lock" maneuver is popular. Its multiple readjustments of application, following gradual rotation of the occiput over an arc of 135 degrees or more to anterior, is done with the DeLee-Simpson forceps.

There are many other procedures, mostly modifications of the aforementioned maneuvers (King, Malhardo, etc.), which may be done with a classical type of forceps. Each added procedure emphasizes the deficiencies of the others, showing that no one procedure is entirely satisfactory. Many of these deficiencies may be eliminated by the use of a special type of forceps. Again, the advantages of the Kielland make it the choice except in some of the simpler cases. When the head is at the outlet, it may respond readily to digital rotation without using the entire hand in the vagina and causing displacement, or it may be small enough to offer no resistance to the Scanzoni.

On the direct occiput posterior the upside down direct application of the Kielland simplifies rotation. Posterior positions occur frequently in pelves with a contraction in the transverse diameter, such as the anthropoid or android types. Descent cannot occur in the transverse. Therefore, anterior rotation is completed first, and then traction is applied. The Kielland is built for this purpose. The Barton is not, since it has no available pelvic curve when the head is anterior.

4. Finally, the occiput posterior may on rare occasions be *delivered as such without anterior rotation*. In certain cases of android and anthropoid pelves with insufficient room to permit anterior rotation, the delivery is completed as an occiput posterior with a Simpson axis-traction type of forceps.

For face presentation the simplest method of delivery with forceps in most cases and the one offering the best results is with the use of the Kielland.

When the chin is in the transverse or posterior position the accurate application without displacement of the head with the Kielland instrument followed by anterior rotation of the chin and then by traction can be done with a single maneuver.

If the chin is directly posterior the method used is the "upside down direct application" of the Kielland to the sides of the face. This is followed by anterior rotation of the chin and traction.

In anterior chin presentations the Kielland forceps may be used or a Simpson type with good axis traction.

The main exceptions to the use of the Kielland on a face

presentation are a flat pelvis or a deformed sacrum requiring
the mechanism of labor for a flat pelvis. Here, with the chin
in transverse arrest, the Barton is again the only available
instrument that can be used safely to give traction in the
required transverse position with descent before anterior
rotation.

On the aftercoming head the advantages of the Piper
forceps make it the choice, with special exceptions for the
Hawks-Dennen and the Kielland.

REFERENCES

AHNQUIST, G.: Delivery of the persistent transverse vertex utilizing
Barton forceps, West, J. Surg. 60:406 (Aug.); 448 (Sept.) 1952.

BACHMAN, C.: The Barton obstetrical forceps; a review of its use in
fifty-five cases, Surg., Gynec. & Obst. 45:805 (Dec.) 1927.

BARTON, L. G., CALDWELL, W. E., and STUDDIFORD, W. E., SR.: A new
obstetric forceps, Am. J. of Obst. & Gynec. 15:16 (Jan.) 1928.

BILL, A. H.: Forceps rotation of the head in persistent occipitoposterior positions, Am. J. Obst. 78:791 (Dec.) 1918.

BILL, A. H.: Modified Scanzoni maneuver, occipitoposterior positions;
Inter. Clin. 1:264, 1929.

————————— A new axis traction handle for solid blade forceps, Am.
J. Obst. & Gynec. 9:606 (May) 1925.

————————— Forceps delivery, Am. J. Obst. & Gynec. 68:245 (July)
1954.

COCHRAN, G. G.: The Pomeroy maneuver (rotary version). An evalu-
ation of results in 200 cases, Brooklyn Hosp. J. 2:155 (July) 1940.

CORNELL, E. L.: Forcep delivery, Surg., Gynec. & Obst. 44:221 (Feb.)
1927.

COSGROVE, R., and WEAVER, O.: An analysis of 1000 consecutive mid
forceps operations, Am. J. Obst. & Gynec. 73:556 (March) 1957.

DANFORTH, D. N., and ELLIS, A.: Mid forceps delivery—A vanishing
art? Am. J. Obst. & Gynec. 86:29 (May 1) 1963.

DANFORTH, W. C.: The treatment of occipitoposterior positions with especial reference to manual rotation, Am. J. Obst. & Gynec. 23:360 (March) 1932.

DAVIS, C. H.: The clinical use of forceps. In Gynecology and obstetrics, Hagerstown, 1934, v. 2, chap. 2, sect. 2, pp. 17-50.

DECKER, W., and HEATON, C.: Barton Obstetric Forceps; an analysis of 277 cases, Am. J. Obst. & Gynec. 61:635 (March) 1951.

————— DICKSON, W. A., and HEATON, C. E.: An analysis of five hundred and forty-seven mid forceps operations, Am. J. Obst. & Gynec. 65:294 (Feb.) 1953.

DeLEE, J. B.: The treatment of occiput posterior position after engagement of the head, Surg., Gynec. & Obst. 46:696 (May) 1928.

DENNEN, E. H.: A new forceps with a traction curve, Am. J. Obst. & Gynec. 22:258 (Aug.) 1931.

DENNEN, E. H.: Manual of forceps deliveries, privately printed, 1947.

————— Choice of instrument in delivery with forceps, New York State J. Med. 32:802 (July) 1932.

————— A classification of forceps operations according to station of head in pelvis. Including results in 3,883 forceps deliveries, Am. J. Obst. & Gynec. 63:272 (Feb.) 1952.

————— The selection of an obstetric forceps to suit the case, Virginia M. Monthly 74:150 (April) 1947.

————— Choice of forceps, Clin. Obst. & Gynec. 2:367 (June) 1959.

————— Selection of instrument for forceps deliveries, with results in 10,405 forceps operations, Berichten—II Weltkongress Fur Gynakologie und Geburtshilfe. Wein. Band I. 44, 1961.

DIECKMANN, WILLIAM J.: The place of operative obstetrics, Am. J. Obst. & Gynec. 69:1005 (May) 1955.

DONALD, IAN: Practical obstetric problems; Textbook: Year Book Publishers 1955—Chapter 19.

DOUGLAS, R. GORDON, AND STROMME, WILLIAM B.: Operative Obstetrics. New York, Appleton-Century-Crofts, 1957.

EADIE, FREDERICK S., and KEETTEL, WILLIAM C.: Trial and failed forceps; Obst. & Gynec., (Aug.) 1954; 4:241-245; Year Book Obstetrics, 1955-56, Pg. 169.

FARRELL, J. R., and DENNEN, E. H.: A review of 527 mid forceps deliveries, Post-Grad. M. J. 11:210 (March) 1952.

FLEMING, A. R., BRANDBERRY, K. R., and PEARSE, W. H.: Introduction of a metric forceps, Am. J. Obst. & Gynec. 78:125 (July) 1959.

GOMEZ, H. E., and DENNEN, E. H.: Face presentation. A study of 45 consecutive cases, Obst. & Gynec. 8:103 (July) 1956.

GOOD, F. L.: A new obstetric forceps, Surg., Gynec. & Obst. 5:342 (Sept.) 1907.

GREENHILL, J. P.: The Kielland forceps, Am. J. Obst. & Gynec. 7:349 (March) 1924.

IRVING, F. C.: The Tarnier axis traction rods applied to the Simpson obstetric forceps, Surg., Gynec. & Obst. 20:734, 1915.

JACOBS, J. B.: Persistent occipitoposterior; a simple and safe method of treatment with the use of new forceps, South. M. J. 29:891 (Sept.) 1936.

JARCHO, J.: The Kielland obstetrical forceps and its application, Am. J. Obst. & Gynec. 10:35 (July) 1925.

JEFFCOATE, T. N. A.: British Medical Journal, 2:951, 1953.

KIELLAND, C.: Direct personal communication and instruction, 1931 and 1937.

——————— Uber die Anlegung der Zange am nicht rotierten Kopf mit beschreibung eines neuen Zangenmodelles, und einer neuen Anlegungsmethode, Monatschr. f. Geburtsh. u. Gynäk. 43:48, 1916.

KING, E. L., HERRING, J. S., DYER, I., and KING, J. A.: The modification of the Scanzoni rotation in management of persistent occipitoposterior positions, Am. J. Obst. & Gynec. 61:872 (April) 1951.

LABRECK, F. A.: Obstetric delivery forceps, Am. J. Surg. 48 (ns):697 (June) 1940.

LANGMAN, L., and TAYLOR, H. C., JR.: The selection of forceps for midpelvic arrest of the vertex, Am. J. Obst. & Gynec. 52:773 (Nov.) 1946.

LAUFE, L. E.: New obstetric forceps, Obst. & Gynec. 7:91 (Jan.) 1956.

LUIKART, R.: A new forceps possessing a sliding lock, modified fenestra, with improved handle and axis-traction attachment, Am. J. Obst. & Gynec. 40:1058 (Dec.) 1940.

———————— A modification of the Kielland, Simpson, and Tucker-McLane forceps to simplify their use and improve function and safety, Am. J. Obst. & Gynec. 34:686 (Oct.) 1937.

MANN, J.: The application of a universal joint to obstetric forceps, Am. J. Obst. & Gynec. 26:399 (Sept.) 1933.

———————— Forceps. In the Cyclopedia of Medicine, Surgery, Specialties. (Philadelphia), F. A. Davis Co., V. 11, pp. 227-246.

———————— Methods for improving the results of forceps deliveries, J. Obst. & Gynec. (Brit. Emp.) 64:351 (June) 1957.

MAUGHN, G. B.: The safe and simple delivery of persistent posterior and transverse positions, Am. J. Obst. & Gynec. 71:741 (April) 1956.

MELHADO, G. C.: The occipitoposterior position, Am. J. Obst. & Gynec. 26:696 (Nov.) 1933.

MISEO, A.: New obstetric forceps with a split universal joint principle, Obst. & Gynec. 8:487 (Oct.) 1956.

MOORE, E. J. T., and DENNEN, E. H.: Management of persistent brow presentations, Obst. & Gynec. 6:186 (Aug.) 1955.

MORGAN & REYES: The case for mid forceps, Am. J. Obst. & Gynec. 69:1193 (June) 1955.

PEARSE, W. H.: Electronic recording of forceps delivery, Am. J. Obst. & Gynec. 86:43 (May) 1963.

PIERI, R. J.: The occipitoposterior position and the modified Scanzoni maneuver, New York State J. Med. 40:1773 (Dec. 15) 1940.

PIPER, E. B.: A new axis-traction forceps, Am. J. Obst. & Gynec. 24:625 (Oct.) 1932.

PIPER, E. B., and BACHMAN, C.: The prevention of fetal injuries in breech delivery, J.A.M.A. 92:217-221 (Jan. 19) 1929.

POSNER, A. C., and COHN, S.: An analysis of forty-five face presentations, Am. J. Obst. & Gynec. 62:592 (Sept.) 1951.

REID, DUNCAN E.: A Textbook of Obstetrics. Philadelphia, W. B. Saunders Co., 1962.

RIEDIGER, K.: Ein Schloss für die Kiellandzange zur Entwicklung toter Kinder nach vorausgegangen Perforation, Zentralbl. für Gynäk. 51:2198 (Aug. 20) 1927.

SCADRON, S. J.: Management of the occipitoposterior position with special reference to the application of the Kielland forceps, Surg., Gynec. & Obst. 40:697 (May) 1925.

SEIDES, S. A.: A "two-forceps maneuver" for persistent occipitoposterior presentation, Surg., Gynec. & Obst. 36:421 (March) 1923.

STUDDIFORD, W. E.: The Barton forceps. New York Sklar Manufacturing Co. 1946.

TATELBAUM, ABRAHAM J.: A method of forceps rotation in posterior positions, Am. J. Obst. & Gynec. 57:553-556 (March) 1949.

TAUBER, R.: Contribution to the technique of the Kielland forceps, Clinics 5:961-970 (Dec.) 1946.

ULLERY, J. C., TETERIS, N. J., BOTSCHNER, A. W., and McDANIELS, BETTY: Traction and compression forces exerted by obstetric forceps and their effect on foetal heart rate, Am. J. Obst. & Gynec. 85:1066 (April 15) 1963.

WEBSTER, J. C., and DAVIS, C. H.: The forceps; historical consideration. In: Gynecology and obstetrics, Hagerstown, 1941, v. 2, chap. 2, section 1, pp. 1-16.

WILLIAMSON, H. C.: Application of the forceps to transverse head for delivery of persistent occipitoposterior cases, Am. J. Obst. & Gynec. 11:37 (Jan.) 1926.

WYLIE, B.: Forceps traction, an index of birth difficulty, Am. J. Obst. & Gynec. 86:38 (May 1) 1963.

Index

NOTE: Page numbers in italics indicate illustrations.

A

Advantages
  Barton forceps, 152
  Kielland forceps, 106
  Piper forceps, 176
After coming head, Piper forceps, 175
  advantages, 176
  construction, 175
  disadvantages, 176
  reason for use, 183
  technic, 176
    application to, about to be delivered over perineum by flexion without removal of forceps, *182*
    during traction, *181*
    insertion from below upward of first (left) blade to right ear of aftercoming head, *178*
    insertion of second (right) blade to left ear of aftercoming head, *179*
Anesthesia for forceps deliveries, 39
Anterior
  asynclitism, causing anterior parietal presentation (L.O.T.), *15*
  chin presentation
    application of Kielland forceps to, ready for traction, after counterclockwise rotation of face presentation, L.M.T. to MA., *146*
    Kielland forceps, 141

Anterior (*Continued*)
  fontanelle, 13, 17
  (left) blade
    introduction of, for R.O.A., *52*
  Kielland forceps
    clockwise rotation in R.O.T. so that its cephalic curve will coincide with curve of head, *132*
    insertion of, to anterior (left) ear of R.O.T. by inversion method, *130*
    opposite anterior (left) ear of R.O.T., *131*
  (left) ear, hinged Barton blade has been "wandered" by index and middle fingers of left hand around right side of pelvis over occiput of flexed R.O.T. to, behind symphysis, *158*
  parietal presentation, high L.O.T., *27*
  parietal presentation (L.O.T.) due to anterior asynclitism, *15*
  (right) blade
    Elliot forceps
      introduction of, for instrumental rotation, L.O.T. to O.A., *78*
      wandering maneuver in application to L.O.T., *79*
    introduction of, in L.O.A., and locking of handles, *45*

217